Of God and Gin

Of God and Gin

Exploring Life, The Universe and Everything
with Meditation & Mindfulness

SALLY BURNLEY

© Sally Burnley, 2017

Published by Starburst Books

A CIP catalogue record for this book is available from the British Library.

ISBN 978-0-9955855-0-8

Book layout and cover design by Clare Brayshaw

Cover images

© Seandnad | Dreamstime.com (Ice & Lemon photo)

© Saknakron | Dreamstime.com (Head of Buddha photo)

Prepared and printed by:

York Publishing Services Ltd
64 Hallfield Road
Layerthorpe
York YO31 7ZQ

Tel: 01904 431213

Website: www.yps-publishing.co.uk

I dedicate this book to a fat, old, dead, rascally Indian man, Neem Karoli Baba. I despised you and you claimed me anyway, for which I am eternally grateful and not a little impressed.

This book takes you through, and explains, different methods of meditation and contemplation, designed to allow you to experience for yourself your true nature, the continuing energy that is you, your own amazing power.

I was once sitting cross-legged across an aisle from a hippie-looking guy for a meditation and afterwards he looked over to me and drawled, "I used to pay a laaata money to feel like this."

Contents

Introduction   ix

Happy?   1

All about compassion   15

Mindfulness, or the cavalry coming over
the hill   27

Let's have a go – Mindfulness Meditation   41

Intention and popular science weirdness   49

A knock-your-socks-off spiritual experience –
the BKs   63

God, the Beard, the Cloud, the Smiting   75

What about Vipassana, insight meditation?   87

Let's do Vipassana. How hard can it be?   103

Who needs a guru?   117

The *Ramayana* for dummies   129

Am I doing it right? Synchronicity and
  pointers along the way   143

They're states Jim, but not as we know them   159

Retreat with scary nun   167

Intention and car parking spaces   177

A contemplation on Awareness and Intention   189

A yawning chasm in reality – help!   203

I can't do any of that! How else can I
  get there?   215

Introduction

It could be just a short attention span, but this lifetime I have been a physiotherapist, lawyer, yoga teacher, knitwear designer and now I am a homeopath, acupuncturist, NST/Bowen practitioner and healer, amongst other things. Along the way I acquired the roles of wife, mother, daughter, the whole ball of wax. I think in the entirety of my journey, I have, in fact, been looking for something else, something ultimately satisfying. I have to report back that I have never found it *out there* in the world. Rather, it appears to be inside. What I am suggesting is that the answer, if you can call it that, is in the very essence of us.

With all that knowledge and life experience, here I am, much the same as I when started. This essence, of who or what I am, is the same, unmoving, constant – as it is for you. We are the unchanging observers of, and also the full-hearted participants in, life.

Looking back, I have on occasion behaved appallingly; maybe you have too. But I have behaved amazingly too, as have you.

Both categories of behaviour have taught me, and made me who I am today, still a work in progress. The ghastly, mean-spirited stuff has had repercussions that have been uncomfortable. The kind, beautiful stuff has been a gift, both to me and to the recipient; the consequences have been bountiful, with a lovely, ongoing sense of ease.

And what I have learned from reflecting on all of it is the importance of compassion, kindness. I can't afford *not* to be kind, none of us can. What an interesting thing then, this learning path. Could it be that life is a feedback device, or mirror? Maybe the world and our lives are the back-drop to our learning, our schoolroom and our curriculum?

My interest lies in the search and looking inside for answers. Even as a child this was the case, although I wasn't aware of it at the time. There were various quirky ways of thinking that I accepted as normal, but in Middle England, where I grew up, they were not. They would have been normal for a Buddhist perhaps, but none of my family had even heard of Buddhism, I suspect.

For example, I was always fascinated about where thoughts came from and how they were formed. No matter how much I focused on them, clearing my mind, the thoughts always sprang up, fully formed, from nowhere. There were spaces between them but the thoughts were substantial with no wispy building blocks of stray, fragmented concepts or half-feelings which could then coalesce into a fully formed thought. I would ask people what they were thinking about now, now, now this second, this split second.

To my childish disappointment, I would get answers like, "Me dinner".

A filling-happy dentist used to be horrified when I refused injections for big, humbug-induced fillings in back molars and instead went somewhere else in my mind where there was no pain.

I even gave myself a lot of grief when very young about a little bump on my scalp. I was convinced this would always be getting cut when they shaved my head, or worse still, if they didn't cut it there would be bristly bits of hair standing up around it. Horrors. Needless to say I had never even seen anyone with a shaven head when I was having these thoughts.

Then there was the recurring sensation I had of falling through endless, vast space, nothingness, with nowhere to stand, nothing to hang on to. I couldn't even close my eyes because there it was. I was terrified. The Doctor harrumphed a bit and that was that. It went away in the end.

I suppose my life was just a touch mad, but whose isn't? I can see now that these experiences were shadows of Buddhist practices, but that penny only dropped much later. I had always just ignored them.

Instead, I tried to conform, as we all do when we are little, to fit in and get on with it, but with a disconcerting detachment from life and its values.

'Is that all it is?' was a familiar refrain in my head.

From this came an interest in, and indeed a yearning for, the metaphysical, coupled with a delight in the physical.

I've had a lifetime of noticing things and people; noticing my own responses; noticing that meditation makes me more skilful; red wine makes me less so. All of this has given me insight into what helps me and what doesn't and also *who* is helped, what level of me that is, physical me or inside me.

We can explore who we think we are, the flesh and blood bit, and also who and what we *actually* are, the essence.

It's an interesting time to be alive, and thanks to instant communication, the insights are easier to get now, hard to miss in fact.

We notice the planet, that what we are doing to it, and our very lives on it, suck, to such an extent that although it is easier than in the past to bury our heads in multiple distractions, we *know* that's not the answer. We can't carry on as if all is well. We now know that it's not.

We can't avoid knowing about the violence and destruction, but maybe this wretched knowledge makes us just that little bit more prepared to look to see what's going on. Why does it happen? Could it change? Could we change it? Could we change ourselves?

We are able to examine how it is for all of us and whilst the result of that examination might be uncomfortable, there are giants like Einstein, Buddha, Milarepa, Ramakrishna, Lao Tzu, Christ, or even my own guru, who had glimpses of the true magnificence that lies behind all form and have reported back.

The force that lies behind the forms, the force that powers it all is mind-blowing and we can approach it, acknowledge it, and even merge with it, as who and what we truly are.

So prepare to blow your mind.

1

Happy?

Walking my dog in the fields in the evening gloom I met an acquaintance, a brisk, horsey lady, with her dog. We hadn't seen each other for a while and began catching up. I mentioned that I had just been on a mini-retreat with a Tibetan Lama, not my usual practice, but this was going on close to home and I do try to get away when I can.

She leant in close to me so as not to be overheard by HH, her hearty husband, a few eloquent paces ahead. "What can meditation do for you?" she asked. "What could it do for me?" Her tone was conspiratorial.

I'd never thought of myself as a secret meditation pusher, but I kept my voice suitably confidential and gave her all the stuff about calming down, observing your thoughts and reactions and so making better decisions – and in my defence, it was all true...

"Would it make me happier?" She cut to the chase.

"Um, yes."

I added that deep down you have a source of happiness and contentment, in fact you *are* that happiness and contentment and with meditation you can access it. I'm not sure she was ready for that, but I gave it to her anyway. I mean, cross, bossy husbands can be tricky to live with, she needed to know.

I could see her predicament, and we all have similar predicaments. We are all looking for the perfect external conditions to make us happy.

But external conditions can't do it for us, because nothing stays the same out there. The dream husband/wife develops gout, halitosis and a bad temper; the desirable house has an incinerator built next door to it; this youthful body ages. So what can we do to maintain our happiness, our joy, in the face of life – or perhaps *find* a bit of joy in the first place?

This courageous woman was looking for a way through as she drew out of me the answer to the question 'Why meditate?'

She was right, it is all about happiness, and contentment, and the fact that they don't stay with you in the world, because things in the world change.

HH was striding towards the horizon now and my friend relaxed. "Isn't it irresponsible," she wondered, "to do what you've been doing? I mean you can't just sit there going inside and smiling – life goes on and it's sad, depressing... and incredibly irritating." She eyed the retreating back.

I agreed that the world was often harsh, grim even. You can acknowledge it all, open to it, but then continually being sad about it isn't going to help, it just adds to the general sadness. Not useful at all.

What would happen if, despite every argument, disappointment and misfortune that was going on, you could stay open and not run away into: being busy so as not to think; judging people and apportioning blame; shopping; making it all someone's fault. What if you could embrace all the messiness of life and still access peace, joy and equanimity? Think of all that extra energy you would free up, the energy you've been pouring into your form of avoidance! (Try not to think of the shoes you would have missed had you not done the shopping thing.)

"Thanks," said my friend with a smile and went off to catch up with HH.

We've all got mess in our lives. But the mess is what's happening in this moment, this is your life, in fact. So running away is running away from your life

Being open to it all and yet still in touch with your inner spaciousness would mean that other people wouldn't be able to hurt you, because you'd have already faced and made peace with all your messy stuff. You'd be relaxed about people's opinions of you, they are just people's opinions, and those people don't really know you. But *you* would know you, and that's what counts.

In this Utopian situation, there would be no need to be fearful and judgemental. If you were in touch with your centre you would probably feel a natural love and compassion for yourself and for the suffering of those critical of you (they've got to be suffering if they're being foul). Your feelings of love and compassion would spread out from you, people would feel better around you, and so react differently. It would benefit you and benefit the world. That's got to be something the world needs, and of course what you need.

Happy breeds more happy.

What meditation shows you is that even though the merry-go-round of life, and your fortunes, are forever changing and challenging, it's OK because happiness, the lasting kind, isn't to be found out there in the first place. It's an inside job, and it is to do with the part of you that doesn't change, the essence of you, what Buddhists would call your true nature.

You have this source of contentment and joy within you, we all do. With meditation, you can make peace with you and your external upsets, quiet down and learn to open to this inner nature. You notice that your spacious nature doesn't depend on what's happening *to* you. It's a constant. Deep down you *are* spacious, peaceful and joyful. You just need to access it.

I was left feeling grateful to my friend for our exchange, it made me think about that inner peace and the fellow-feeling, or compassion, for others, for the person in front of us and for ourselves. Could meditation help us find our happiness and compassion? And could it help us in our lives? My experience is that it can help and it does. In fact, it transforms the whole game.

I tend to be an explorer rather than a joiner and have spent a lifetime exploring meditation techniques (and jobs, you may have noticed from the Introduction). I have been constantly surprised at the connections between all the techniques and practices I've experienced. None are an unapproachable mystery and one may even turn out to be the perfect practice for you.

THE JOURNEY BEGINS IN THE GYM

In my growing up I was aware of jumbled, chaotic thoughts, bringing every anxiety and excitement to rattle my cage, whether I wanted those thoughts or not. From being an anxious, eager-to-please child I progressed to being a self-conscious, far-too-nice child then to a somewhat wild and tortured teenager – you know the story line.

When I was about 25yrs old, and a trainee lawyer, I heard about yoga from the office junior. I was fascinated, and thought it would be a way to calm my racing mind.

So off I went to the grubby gymnasium of the local comprehensive school where the teacher was a lovely dumpy lady in a holey leotard and a cardy (forget fluorescent Lycra with dazzling tights, this was a long time ago in freezing cold Yorkshire). She was putting us through extraordinary contortions, which made me feel strangely alive and good. I loved the breathing and gentling into the poses and most of all I loved the relaxation at the end.

We would wrap ourselves up in woolly hats and outdoor coats and lie down on our camping mats whilst doing a breathing and relaxation exercise culminating in this unlikely lady waggling the phrase at us: "I will bring peace to my mind, peace." This came along with the sweaty sock aroma of the gym.

I was amazed by the calming effect of the breathing and basic yoga practice. But I knew there was more, so I sat with the teacher on a low form, worn shiny from so many children's velour-clad bottoms, and she gave me a reading list of Hindu texts plus a bad attack of vegetarianism which lasted for 15 years.

In fact, I was a *vegan* for the year before I conceived my first child, which hugely upset my obstetrician, not least because I looked healthier than he did. We compromised by adding bone meal tablets into the mix as I recall – horrors, an animal product. It was good obviously, made my diet, and me, a teensy bit less obsessional.

TRANSCENDENTAL MEDITATION

It was during that pregnancy that I started to meditate.

I was concerned. The hay-fever season was approaching and I didn't want to take hay-fever drugs whilst pregnant. I knew that stress had a bearing on allergies so wondered if meditation would lower the stress levels enough to stop my symptoms.

It was the time of Transcendental Meditation (TM) and The Beatles. I popped off to a local TM centre to be initiated.

I'm afraid to say that I found it hugely funny.

I felt silly clutching a bunch of wilting Michaelmas daisies and, with no shoes and socks on, going in to see a large Indian man dressed in a sheet sitting in a throne-like chair, with me sitting on the floor at his feet. I remember wondering if it was a set up for *Candid Camera*, I felt so daft. I was then given a mantra, a single word, to repeat to myself and not divulge to anyone else. (Of course, I was convinced that everyone was given the same word and that it was all a complete con.)

I think I handed over the cash to a front man in an outer vestibule and left feeling vaguely discomfited.

Not an auspicious start on my meditation journey.

Still, I'd paid my dosh and with nothing to lose I said my mantra as instructed. And sure enough, to my astonishment, I did get much more peaceful. Peaceful Mum, peaceful baby, it was all lovely.

Oh, and no hay-fever. It worked!

I pursued TM for some time but ultimately became dissatisfied, as it didn't seem to be going anywhere spiritually. And when the next step was to be an advanced practice called Yogic Flying where you seemed to bounce around the room on your bottom trying to get airborne, I abandoned it.

I could see that if your mind became perfectly focused and one-pointed, miracles like levitation could happen, but that surely shouldn't be the *object* of the exercise. I wanted the focus, the one-pointedness, but I wanted to use it to see through the game, to find out what life was about, not to have a showy power. I felt that a glitzy power like levitation would be a side-alley, and instead of going to the light I'd spend a lifetime showing off and being a levitator. I had enough labels in my life I wanted to cut through all my stuff, not acquire more.

I sort of forgot about TM and carried on with yoga, which I was teaching by now, having done, during my pregnancy, a British Wheel of Yoga teaching course, run by my same lovely teacher.

After the birth, I started a class in the village hall where I then lived, on the edge of moorland, in an even colder part of Yorkshire. I still particularly loved the mini-meditation and relaxation bit at the end and would focus on the overflowing love I felt for the jumble of people who braved the hall every week.

They loved it too, and two cyclists (with amazingly stiff bodies) were heard to say in a spaced-out sort of way, "You wouldn't think you'd find all this in a village hall, would you?"

I think what they found was that compassion, unconditional positive regard, love. A sort of spiritual glue.

Compassion is always in the mix no matter what meditation technique you start with. It's a spiritual given, revealed when you practice and it can be a practice in its own right. *Compassion*, and, because it makes you feel so good, naturally arising *gratitude*, are always there.

Then came a milestone in my life when I got a glimpse of my own path and true compassion.

ME AND MY CERVIX

My doctor became alarmed because of a growth on my cervix. I was sent to a consultant the same day (you know it's serious when you see someone the same day). I said to the consultant that if she needed to operate on me the next day to save my life then so be it, but otherwise I would like two weeks to try and heal it myself.

This was grudgingly agreed and I got hold of a bloke who was a hypnotist. I'd figured that, having had a couple of pelvic problems, it must be a sex thing. I wanted the guy to regress me to being tiny and read a little prepared script to me as if he were my mother. The script was all about the joys and fun of sex and loving relationships without my mother's underlying subtext of paranoia about unwanted pregnancies and disease.

It was decided that I would close my eyes and meditate and he would do all his hypnotic suggestion. The pointer on the dial of the biofeedback device on my wrist would then move from the vertical to a few degrees left. He would know I was hypnotised and stop using a silly voice.

There was a hitch because as soon as I started to meditate the needle went off the scale to the left so he thought he wouldn't be able to hypnotise me. It was agreed that my meditation state would do the job, so I just meditated and he regressed away as if I were hypnotised.

His line was: "Going back, where are you now…" I found myself in a sun-filled room with my mother and the script was read to me. "Going back, where are you now…" He was exceeding his brief, taking me further back, but I mentally shrugged and let it carry on.

I found myself standing on a large sloping rock on a hillside in high rugged mountains. I immediately thought how very clever of me, because I was probably making it up and you couldn't date this as there were no buildings and no people. He asked me questions that I found useless and couldn't answer: what was I wearing, how old was I, who were my parents, did I live with them and any brothers and sisters? I didn't get any of it.

Then he asked me what sex I was and I paused then grinned broadly. The bloke said, "You've just looked!" and I had, I was wearing a brownish robe and I'd pulled it out and looked down, I saw male genitalia, a penis, naked, with no hair. It was such a shock.

I continued to be flummoxed by his questions and found myself feeling huge love and sympathy for him. What I noticed was his tangled, confused mind and realised that my own mind was calm and still; it was vast and tranquil like a huge lake surface on a windless day.

I realised that I was a young monk and I lived in a monastery and not with a family. I dismissed this story instantly and again thought I was making it up, maybe I wanted to be a monk or something, though as a young mother of two, it was nowhere on my list of aspirations.

But then there was this love and good-wishes I felt for him, arising from a calm, clear, limpid mind. I had never experienced anything thing like that in this lifetime, so couldn't have imagined it.

Now that was interesting.

It still intrigues me, that compassion I felt for him, with his jumping, limited mind.

It was a bit bonkers, I mean, *he* was supposedly helping *me*.

When I went back to the consultant, the lump had gone. Everything was 'as clean as a whistle'. She looked confused even a little cross. She didn't ask me what I'd done to heal it, but then I doubt I could have told her.

But the story turns a spotlight on compassion. Are you capable of it, and what can it do for you? We will explore the wonderfulness of compassion, how it can add a massive dimension to your life – simply put, it makes you feel better, happier. And we can begin to experience it for ourselves with a simple loving-kindness meditation.

2

All about compassion

At the end of a Tibetan Buddhist retreat the teaching Lama had gone outside with some of the retreatants. A young man with complicated facial hair and a beanie, who was just visiting the venue, came in through the door.

'That man," he said to me, nodding back to the Lama, "is he a monk?"

"Yes," I said.

"I've never met a monk before. He's... He was behind me and I just felt this feeling," he touched his heart. "He's amazing."

And they are, it's the compassion they practice.

The Dalai Lama is interested in science. He allowed some of his monks to have their brains tested and the prefrontal cortex of each of them was greatly enlarged.

Now the frontal lobe of the brain is what separates us from the rest of the animal world, what makes us human. It makes us civilised and gives us our personalities. It is the seat of our emotions, gives us discrimination, empathy and the ability to put ourselves in the other's shoes. Also it enables us to run through a scenario before we enact it so we don't just barge ahead heedlessly. It enables us to make decisions and control our impulses.

Interestingly, Attila the Hun had his head bound in infancy, squashing the front of he skull, so his head came to a point. There would have been very little room for the prefrontal cortex. He would have looked terrifying and certainly seemed to be lacking in the compassion department!

Anyway, the practice of compassion actually enlarges this wonderful bit of the brain, making us all the more human. You begin to see how compassion could be good for you.

Practices of compassion start very simply, anyone can do them, and a great incentive is that although it looks as if you practice this compassion *for another*, the person who gets the benefit primarily is *you*. The other person may feel better or not, but you certainly do. (Later you come to the realisation that we are interconnected and the giving to another becomes reward enough, and such a joy. But an initial 'me, me, me' is fine.)

Most meditation practices include compassion. Let's plunge in.

HOW DOES COMPASSION WORK?

Part of our predicament is that we believe we are separate from everybody else, and so we are alone – in a great big universe. It's scary, and of course, lonely.

Compassion can help.

Being frightened and alone means we suffer, and, by extension, so does everyone else, as they too feel frightened and alone in a great big universe.

Compassion is about being with another in *their* suffering, *with love*. It brings us close to the other and puts us in their shoes. We share their emotion (compassion means 'with passion' – with their passion), we are one with them and as a result, bingo, we are no longer alone. (Phew, what a relief!)

In contrast, you could be with another's suffering with *fear* instead of love. That's the one where you are sort of sorry for them but secretly quite fearful and glad it's them and not you. This would produce pity, which is distancing you from them and it compounds their isolation and your own. So you're alone in a great big universe – again.

Pity doesn't help, compassion does.

I try to use compassion when I'm, say, angry. I like to feel good, and I notice that anger makes me feel hot and horrible inside. So that anger isn't serving me well.

I then notice that I am usually angry about a specific something or someone.

It's their *fault*. I am filling with anger and pouring anger into them. Now they may or may not feel it, but I certainly do and it's no good for me; it's initially exhilarating, but totally draining and will make me ill in the long run, think of the blood pressure!

So instead I haul myself back, if I can, and practice compassion instead. I consider the whole situation, the predicament, and allow compassion to arise, for all of us. I begin to see why *they* (the perceived enemy) are doing it, putting myself in their shoes. I see why *my* buttons are being pushed – having compassion for me too, being gentle with myself for my rather mean-spirited, vitriolic response.

Then it starts to calm down and I begin to feel better.

I know this is obvious but it came as a blinding light for me: if I can't do anything about it, it's pointless getting cross; and if I can do something about it, I do – so it's pointless getting cross.

Also, the things I do out of anger are usually ill-judged, inappropriate, temper-fuelled and swift, they get me into all sorts of bother, whereas the calm energy of compassion is more sustained and I come up with better solutions, or acceptance.

As I revel in the other person's awfulness and my own self-righteousness, I notice that I have to keep stoking the embers of hate to feed my indignation, just to keep it going, it's hard work, and a little pointless. It's almost a relief to try understanding and compassion, when, strangely, the enemy becomes a person just like me, just wanting to be happy. Then things seem to work out.

So compassion, and its concomitant, loving kindness, may be great to receive, but even if you think the perceived enemy is not *open* to receiving it, not in a million years (because the bastards are just too awful, obviously) it clearly has the most incredible effect on the giver – and that's you. Yippee.

The Tibetans make the practice of compassion a cornerstone of all they do. Because, in fact, ultimately it helps the heart let go of its grabbing and what they call the 'self-cherishing' of the ego, the individual self – me, me, me. Giving to others is a gift to us all.

It may start as a practice to help you feel good, but if you did nothing else as a practice it would probably see you through to enlightenment and you'd be great to be around.

The importance the Tibetan Buddhists place on compassion was illustrated by a TV interview with a Tibetan monk who had escaped over the Himalayas to India and was being greeted by the Dalai Lama. He had been tortured every day by the Chinese before he escaped and he said, "I was in terrible danger". From the safety of my comfortable sofa, I thought, yes you were. But he hadn't finished his sentence. He continued, "I was in terrible danger... of losing my compassion for the Chinese."

Wow, that told me.

DEVELOPING COMPASSION

This is more of a gentle *exploration* than a meditation. Be quiet and calm, allow yourself to go with the thoughts.

Consider all of the people on the planet and realise how very similar they are to you.

We are not doing what we usually do which is to note all the differences between others and ourselves and then judge them on the differences. We are looking for the similarities. Do they all have roughly the same number of limbs as us, the same internal organs, the same bodily needs?

You see that all these people want to be happy as do you, and have a fear of suffering as do you. They all move towards pleasure and away from pain, and so do you.

Think about the people close to you and observe that this is true for them, and that it explains their behaviour. They are wanting happiness, they want to avoid suffering. The husband who is overworking is avoiding the pain of job loss or poverty. The bad driver is maybe avoiding the consequences of being late for work or his appointment.

Consider the people in power who are insecure and who fear for their powerful positions, the pain of having a self-esteem that says I have to be important to be worthy, consider the motivations of people and see how similar they all are, and how similar they are to your own motivations.

Think of someone whose actions have distressed you and acknowledge that there is more that is the same between you and them than is different.

Now try to put yourself, as vividly as you can, in his or her place. See the pressures and pulls on them, get a feel for why they behave the way they do. Feel the fears that drive them.

When you exchange yourself for the other in this way you extend your love away from your own needs, self-cherishing, to the needs of the other, the cherishing of the other.

This releases the stranglehold of selfishness on your heart and allows compassion to flow.

Notice that this exchanging yourself for another will not bring on you all their suffering. It doesn't work like that. They may feel nice because of the love coming their way, and you feel wonderful because you have opened your heart and your energy, your *qi*, is flowing – and that heals you. If anything, you feel gratitude to them, it is because of them you are growing and filling with love. And you may even discover a practical action to help the situation.

Recoiling in horror or sadness is about you and your *fear*, compassion is about them and your *love*.

Allow compassion to flow to all beings, all struggling and all doing their best as they perceive it.

Notice that by sending compassion you are no longer the needy person craving the crumbs of others' affection, no longer the victim, you are the person who can give love.

How cool are you?

A LOVING KINDNESS PRACTICE

Sitting comfortably, in a chair or cross-legged on a cushion, make sure that your back is straight and have your hands loosely in your lap with your eyes gently closed.

Bring to mind someone whom you love, it could be a family member, mother, father, sibling, child or possibly the family dog. Imagine that person or animal in front of you. Feel the love arise in you. So simple and easy, it almost comes unbidden.

Send them that love.

May you be happy, may you be free from suffering and the causes of suffering.

Hold them in you loving heart.

After a little time, let that image fade.

Now imagine in front of you someone who is neutral, someone you don't know very well. It could be someone on the bus, the checkout assistant at the supermarket, someone about whom you do not have strong feelings.

Note how similar they are to you, how similar their aspirations, wanting to be happy, wanting not to suffer. Allow your heart to open to them, sending them love.

May you be happy, may you be free from suffering and the causes of suffering.

Let that image fade.

Now imagine the enemy. Someone with whom you have 'unfinished business', that rotter, that blot on the landscape. If you can't think of anyone in your life, just think of an image from the TV news, that will do it.

Instead of hating or becoming overwhelmed, both of which are fear responses, realise that this person is indeed a person, just like you, not an alien other. They want to be happy, just like you, they want to move away from suffering, just like you.

They have been fed a different storyline this lifetime, with life experiences bearing perhaps little similarity to your own, and they see things differently to you, but basically their motivations are the same.

Try opening your heart for a change, we know where judging and hatred will get us. We are familiar with that and we've had quite enough of it.

Opening your creaking heart, send them love. What have you got to lose? They won't even know you're doing it, and I won't tell:

May you be happy, may you be free from suffering and the causes of suffering.

Well done. Now you could give yourself a break and go back to the family dog.

May you be happy, may you be free from suffering and the causes of suffering.

Gently open your eyes and see if your stress levels have reduced!

Homework: Send out loving kindness twice a day and focus on anyone who pops into your mind as you do the practice, being with them in their suffering, and wishing them well.

A TONGLEN PRACTICE

This Tonglen practice is fabulous for using all the negative thoughts that assail you during your day, to good effect. It's easy to do because your thoughts change like the wind, so you only need to wait a while until a negative one comes along.

Guilt and shame are pretty regular visitors in our culture. I know I do little actions all the time that I don't like, little mean-spirited things or even great big whoppers that would shock my granny. Thoughts about these actions come back into my mind and I want to run away from them.

The practice is actually not to run away from them but to look at these negative thoughts, and the attendant negative emotions, in a kindly way.

You're only a fearful human and you do rubbish things sometimes.

Stay with the ghastly thoughts. The Buddhists call this 'calm abiding'. We will do more of this when we do our Mindfulness practice (you will find a lot of these practices have huge similarities).

The idea with Tonglen, however, is to breathe your guilt and your ghastliness, into your spacious loving heart and then breathe out forgiveness for yourself, and also forgiveness for all other beings who have behaved in similar ways, and who also feel shame and guilt.

After doing that for a few breaths you feel much better and you don't have to run away from the thoughts and emotions any more by shopping, drinking and TV watching. In fact, you feel relaxed and good, you've made friends with some of your rather negative stuff.

The clever bit is that you are using your human frailty to connect you with the rest of humanity and wishing all of us frail humans well, with compassion and forgiveness. Your nasty bits turn out to be a chance to be compassionate with yourself and with others.

Well, there had to be some good use for all that guilt.

3

Mindfulness, or the cavalry coming over the hill

As I was having some energy work done on me recently, I was brooding on several things, injustices, things that shouldn't have happened, to me or to my loved ones. To say that I wasn't relaxed was an understatement, the therapist pointed out that my shoulders were up by my ears somewhere with the muscles of my neck like bands of steel. Then another instance of gross unfairness came into my mind and I burned with indignation and outrage.

It was early, on a beautiful morning, and I was lying quietly on a couch in a perfectly peaceful setting, this was ridiculous.

Checking in with my body I could feel it all in my chest: anger, grief, despair, hopelessness. I'd got the lot. I knew it was impossible to relax with all this going on in my life, my head and my body. I wanted to jump off the couch and come back another day (to get busy and run away from my thoughts, you notice). Then I realised that all the different stories of injustice and sadness that I found so intolerable were just that, *just stories*, and the common denominator in all of them was *me*, and my mind.

I knew I could choose not to take the thoughts so seriously, just relax with them. Life and thoughts are constant changing, and by trying to stop the change you suffer, and I was suffering.

What if I were to stop analysing, planning, plotting and grieving? Just notice it all, and, well, stop. Hmmm, I could try.

Right, I paid massive, mindful attention to the *feelings* in my chest, without their stories, my judgements and worries (I'd just like to point out here though that the protagonists in those stories *were* all in the wrong, obviously).

Very reluctantly I started to let go of the stories and judgements and how right I was (and how wrong they all were). I began to focus on the feelings there in my chest trying to be at peace with the feelings, love them even. Some hope, I was still burning, but mindfully. Forcing myself, I considered the comfort of the couch I was on, my breathing, the efforts of the practitioner and before I knew it my body was relaxing down, sinking into the bench, what a relief! The fight was over.

So how did that happen? Mindfulness.

(This exploration of Mindfulness is out of synch with my life's meditation experiences, but Mindfulness is very popular now and in case it's what you're really looking for, I decided not to leave it in Chapter 15 in case you abandoned hope before you got there.)

You can see how useful Mindfulness could be, I mean I went from screwed up to peaceful in no time at all; no wonder the world is interested.

Mindfulness is wonderfully calming, it's easy, and may be a good starting point for you. It has some links with Buddhist practice but is incredibly practical and accessible now.

So here goes.

WHAT IS MINDFULNESS?

Mindfulness is noticing what's going on. We notice the random parade of thoughts and emotions and their effects in the body with a sort of kindly acceptance. We stop fighting them.

Mindfulness is not hell-bent on your transcending life's troubles, so much as helping you to become aware of what is troubling you right now, without running away.

Just noticing how the body *feels* in the midst of your surroundings and your busy life – and it can be a bit of a shock at first.

This is because we usually ignore our internal goings on, tending to be quite hard on the body, expecting it to cope with all kinds of stresses, and then becoming alarmed or cross when it breaks down in some way.

Getting ready to go and play some sport recently, I suddenly stopped as I was rushing around, late again. I paused, looked inside and asked my body 'how is this for you?' It was, in fact, pants.

Because I was running late, my mind was racing, I was anxious and uptight and my body was registering it. My heart was pounding, with my stomach tense and in a knot. It was crazy.

So much for the health benefits of sport, I thought, there clearly weren't many health benefits to be found in *getting ready* for sport, at least not the way I was doing it.

Just that checking-in with the body reinforced the obvious: I needed to allow an extra ten minutes to get ready in future and not fill my time up to the wire. That would be much more relaxing, and very practical for maintaining the health of my body as well as my mind, whilst admittedly not getting the dishwasher emptied.

I had just become more mindful, and perhaps it would help.

SO HOW DO YOU DO IT?

Sitting quietly, you first pay attention to the internal state of the body, really noticing how the body feels. You notice any troublesome thoughts, any negative emotions and any attendant unpleasant physical feelings. Then without judging, you can switch our attention to the breath, usually in the abdomen – the abdomen rising on the in-breath and falling on the out-breath. Just breathing, in and out. It's so simple, so familiar, it grounds you in the present moment.

Breathing. There is always the breath, safe, present. You watch the rising and falling of the abdomen as a respite from all manner of scary feelings in the body. The breath feels good, not going anywhere, it has known parameters, it's peaceful. You can choose the breath in this moment.

You can then widen your attention to take in the whole body, the contact with the chair or the floor, the physical sensations in the legs, trunk, head, etc.

And suddenly it's OK, the bigger picture starts to loosen the emotional knots, it puts your internal stuff into a wider context.

That's the basic thing.

THAT MIND, THOSE THOUGHTS

You begin to notice the passing parade of your thoughts. You notice the emotions created by your thoughts, especially your stressful ones. You become adept at spotting these emotions, and their effects in the body, the sensations, giving them attention, not with a view to changing anything, rather you have a kindly interest. It's what is, in this moment.

And of course you haven't been doing this, you have been running away from your unpleasant or stressful thoughts, emotions and attendant body tensions.

What you resist persists. Fighting, suppressing or running away from your stressful thoughts and emotions will make them stronger.

Say, you are going to sleep but are feeling restless. You check in with your mind only to find worries bubbling away about a big meeting or presentation tomorrow. You might notice a tension in your stomach, a tingle in your chest. Instead of suppressing or fighting the worries and sensations you could then welcome them (the mind is trying to help by bringing all this to you). You could acknowledge that the worries are there and are all about the future, fully accept the discordant feelings in the body. And then you could widen your focus to other things happening in the moment, less stressful things.

You could perhaps become aware of the feel and weight of the duvet, the softness of the pillow, the evenness of your breath. And so sleep is much more likely; you don't have to stay awake for the fight with the worries, the fight with the worries is over. Because you focused on them fully, the worries have been attended to.

After I wrote this example of Mindfulness I had a great synchronistic experience:

Before coming down to write some more, I was lying on a mat on my bedroom floor doing some Pilates and was in the moment, peaceful. I had the window open and could hear birdsong and the distant hum of traffic.

I was doing the practice of being mindfully aware of sound, not judging it, not creating a story round it, just being with the sensation of sound. Suddenly there was a really loud radio playing close to the window outside, with a lot of jokey conversation on, it was Radio 2 and Chris Evans, and it was *so loud*, I could hear every word. I was about to get up and close the window, rather judgementally, when I decided *not* to be judgemental about the noise, just be mindful again and notice it as part of what was happening.

I left the window open and accepted the noise. They then played a great track and I did my Pilates in time with the beat.

After the music track, Chris Evans started to interview, at full volume naturally, someone who was talking about the practice of Mindfulness as an aid to sleep! No kidding! I could hear each word clearly and it fitted in with the sleep example above. Thank you, Universe.

Back to the chase:

Over time any thoughts and feelings that you have been pushing away, will have become stronger. In becoming more powerful, they become your habitual thoughts and feelings. But once you shine the bright light of consciousness on them the whole mess loses both its menace and its power over you. It doesn't frighten you anymore, because you can look at it. The mess may even dissipate, though this is not your aim.

By focusing on the thoughts and then the duvet (or whatever is happening in the moment) the stressful thoughts are defused. And if it all gets too much there is always the fall-back position of focusing on the breath. There's no particular technique involved, just notice that your abdomen rises on the in-breath and falls on the out-breath, there is no emotion attached to it.

The practice is simple. You pay attention to thoughts, emotions and sensations in the body. You stay with them calmly, don't attach a story to them. Just notice how it really is.

If that gets too uncomfortable, switch to noticing the breath. The breath is calming. It's nice to know that the breath is always available to calm you down when meditating, or at any point in your day.

And you are practicing to do just that, to get into the habit and cultivate the ability to switch your thinking away from nightmare thoughts and 'what-ifs' to the safety of the breath. It's your 'get out of jail free' card.

You can pick up the cascade of negativity and discomfort at any stage: there is first thought, then emotion and lastly bodily sensation, and any of these can be noticed by you. What you notice may not be pleasant. It's OK to feel it, and even OK not to like it, but it is good to pay kindly attention to it because it's your reality, your life, how it is for you right now.

Don't get too involved in your negative thoughts. Your thoughts are not the truth anyway, even those thoughts that say they are. Believing your negative thoughts gets you into all sorts of bother.

You also notice another thing the mind does. When there is an emotion, instead of allowing it to be around and then pass away again naturally, the mind desperately searches for the *cause* of the emotion. It dredges up every untoward event in the last 20yrs that has given you emotions like this. And you end up feeling dreadful, reliving goodness-knows-what and blaming your mother.

This is the 'doing' mind and it's actually trying to help by bringing all this stuff to you.

But the idea is to go into the 'being' mind. Just be. Be with what is, right now. It's a huge relief, not having to change how things are. So what's happening? Maybe it's feeling grass beneath your feet if you are outside, or the sight of the trees brushing the sky, the sound of cars on the road, the smell of the flowers, the sound of children shouting, faraway laughter. It's all just as it is. And strangely enough, it is rather wonderful in the stillness of this moment, this crevice in time. So awareness can transform a mundane moment of average, work-a-day negativity into a sublime experience of now. And you'd have missed it.

Mindful awareness of now, welcoming everything, and you can't live in the next moment anyway, only in this one.

Thich Nhat Hanh a delightful Vietnamese Zen Buddhist monk came over from his home in France to conduct a retreat in Devon where I met him. He practiced paying attention to thoughts and even transforming neutral thoughts into positive ones, to teach us to be content with how it is now. I can remember him saying, "No' having toothache is a won'ful thing." So how wonderful is grass beneath your feet or birdsong or a big rumbling bus?

You find yourself being so grateful, try it and see for yourself, and that gratitude encourages love for the practice.

The practice is about being with it, everything, as it is, not looking for a reason, just being, here, now, human beings not human doings.

Acceptance of, and surrender into, how it is right now. Moment by moment.

Which sounds remarkably like a path to enlightenment. The mystics would love it. But this is so practical, matter of fact and grounded.

You learn to be kind to yourself and your thoughts, including your thoughts about others. You can then afford to be more open and loving with all those others (woops, there's that compassion thing again).

And rather magically, overall, you will find your stress and anxiety being replaced by rising optimism and a sense of wellbeing. Any negative thought, emotion or sensation is noted and by now there is an increased awareness of this moment – what's going on – and the breath, when in a tight spot. This moment, including the breath, becomes a habit and a friend.

As we've said, Mindfulness works for reducing your stress. As an extra bonus it is a great starting point for going on to explore other spiritual practices, all of which require a focused mind, to some degree.

You notice what a great biofeedback device the body is, showing us through our physical sensations what our thoughts and emotions have been.

Your mind is thinking, it's what minds do. It just scoots all sorts of thoughts before you. In this practice, you are not stopping negative thoughts, you are stopping *believing* them, and so you are not escalating them.

You can let it all be. You can view it all fondly, and enjoy the ride. This is the ride of your life. The cutting edge of creation.

We have created this life from our thoughts, the observer affecting the experiment, as we will see in the New Physics section later.

If every thought has its effect on us, we can use this to work for, and not against, our wellbeing. Life could be different if our negative thinking lost some of its power because we were not resisting it. Imagine being able to see our catastrophic thinking for what it is, just thoughts. Imagine being able to chuckle and say, 'woops, anxiety again', or 'come on in *fear of poverty*, you familiar visitor, sit down, have a cup of tea'. And there's always the breath.

Also, why would you bother to get lost in negative states when you know they can't last and will be replaced by something else, positive or negative, in a trice. You could even choose to enjoy the positive states a bit more, coming into the moment and being happy.

Osho was a spiritual teacher in India who had a fund of good stories, he told of a master who laughed all his life and was laughing even on his deathbed. When asked by a disciple why he was laughing even on his deathbed, he explained that he had realised as a young monk that this was his life and he could choose to be sad or blissful every day. So every morning he chose the blissful option. Why wouldn't he?

Why wouldn't we?

4

Let's have a go –
Mindfulness Meditation

Settle yourself in a meditation posture, sitting on a chair with the feet firmly on the floor or cross-legged on a cushion on the floor. Try to have the back straight and self-supporting, the body comfortable and awake.

(We will focus on a sitting practice here – fewer moving parts – rather than a slow, mindful-movement meditation. But Mindfulness of movement is of great value too.)

BREATH

Be aware of the body in contact with the chair or cushion, surrender the body into gravity, feel it gently anchoring your body, just as it is.

Allow your focus to rest on the breath as it rises and falls in the abdomen, the abdomen rising and swelling on the in-breath and falling and contracting on the out-breath.

Enjoy the comfort of the breath, enjoy the feeling of expansion and contraction.

Notice that the whole body seems subtly to expand on the in-breath and contract on the out-breath, as if there were a subtle ebb and flow of breath and energy. Enjoy the sensation.

If you become aware that your thoughts have wandered, be kind to yourself, notice and accept the thoughts, take a moment to be aware of where they've taken you, and any anxiety they bring, be open to it all. Congratulate yourself on waking up, becoming cognisant of what was happening, and return to the breath and the body sitting on the cushion.

SOUNDS

Be aware of where you are, be aware of the sounds in the room. Open your focus to notice sounds as they come to you from the front, the sides, the back, above and below. Notice your tendency to attach a story to each sound. Notice how you judge the sound as good or bad, the story as good or bad. Just go back to the raw sound, the ability of things to make sounds, the ability of your ear to hear.

Be aware of the sensation of sound, raw vibration in the air touching the eardrum, notice how quickly your mind then interprets this as sound, extracts meaning from the sound and makes up a story about it, in nanoseconds. Notice.

Just go back to the sound.

Ebbing and flowing; different sounds; sounds within sounds; different pitches of sound; different rhythms. Just sounds.

If the mind goes away into a story, notice it and welcome the mind doing what it does. Now welcome the mind becoming aware, going back to the breath to anchor you in this moment.

Returning to sound. The miracle of vibration and sound.

THE INVENTIVE MIND

Then change your focus and become aware of your thoughts as if they were passing stories, travelling across the clear sky of the mind. Notice that they arise, float across the sky and then fade. Notice the passing show, the inevitability of the mind making up stories, thoughts.

Always returning to the anchor of the breath if you notice that the stories have taken you away.

Notice the emotions that arise with the thoughts.

Notice the effects of the emotions in the body. Sit with the emotions, cradle them in your awareness with kindness and compassion, notice them, love them. They are not good or bad, they are simply what is happening now. They are your reality right now in this moment.

Return to the breath or stay conscious of the emotion and watch it lose its power, dissipate and fade, perhaps to be taken over by another thought and emotion. Maybe this new thought is urgent, or it could be in the background, inconsequential stories making easy progress across the mind.

Enjoy the mind, the inventiveness. The continual manufacturing process of the mind.

Be aware of the breath, the body, the senses, the constant input of the mind, the constant judging and discriminating. Gently welcoming it all and allowing it all to be as it is, moment to moment.

You are awake, aware, enjoying the experience of the passing show.

You are exploring yourself, how it is for you. Notice your tendency to push away the negative, stressful thoughts and your attempts to try to hang onto pleasant thoughts.

Just notice. Be alive, in this moment.

KINDNESS

Consider a friend, someone who represents the people you know and like. Invite your friend into your awareness.

Notice your friend may not look like you but also notice how similar you are. Your friend is breathing in and out, just like you, sitting or standing, hearing and seeing. Your friend has thoughts and emotions, registering in the mind and body.

Your friend has a tendency to push away the unpleasant and grasp at the pleasant, just like you.

By knowing yourself so well you can know your friend. You can know the whole world.

Now expand your awareness to the house you are in, all the people in it, the whole neighbourhood and people there. Notice that they are just like you, breathing in and out, desiring the pleasant, averse to the unpleasant.

Breathing, just rest in breathing, the now.

Extend your awareness to the country, to the planet, to all beings, all creatures, all things breathing in and out, respiring, just like you.

With every breath: breathe in empathy with all beings, the predicament of being on the planet, and with the out-breath, breathe out compassion and kindliness.

Breathing in and out with all beings, acknowledging the similarities, the whole planet, the whole of existence, just like you, bathed in kindliness and love. Enjoy the love, the kindness, soften into the exquisite joy of compassion and at-one-ness.

Just breathing, easy, loving.

~

Allow your focus to come back into the room, to your body, sitting, peaceful.

Allow your consciousness to become fully aware of now and how it is for you.

Gently move your fingers and toes, deepen your breathing. Smile and take any insight gained into your life with you, together with the breath.

5

Intention and popular science weirdness

When I was at the beginning of my spiritual journey I noticed that as I focused on my silent mantra for TM, or on my breathing in yoga, things changed. I did become surprisingly calm, I was happier. It didn't always last but I still liked it. I wanted to know more. I wanted to explore where my mind could go, I wanted to know what the sages and mystics of old were talking about.

I knew that in India there were people who developed great powers, pushing sharp objects through their skin, or their cheeks, lying down on a bed of nails, with no pain, no blood and no after-effects. How?

I knew that these people practiced meditation in the form of devotion and surrender to many different deities. They all seemed to have their own path, guru or god. But there were so many deities and gurus that it was confusing to the untutored eye. I felt reluctant to join in, to find out more. I loved what I read in the *Bhagavad Gita* or the *Upanishads*, which had been part of my yoga reading list, but the panoply of gods out there was confusing. I wondered how such a multiplicity could be necessary. And how did you know which one was for you?

This was not my culture. It didn't feel quite right. I was managing the TM and yoga, but they seemed like deodorised Western versions of Hindu practices. Did I have to venture further in, to invest in the beads, open-toed sandals and floaty frocks in order to get answers? Not in a Yorkshire winter, surely.

Continuing my search I began reading more and a friend recommended a book, *The Tao of Physics* by Fritjof Capra. In it Capra repeatedly put two statements in italics and you had to guess which one was a statement by an ancient mystic and which by a quantum physicist. Each time they were practically the same, you couldn't tell them apart.

Wow. I started to explore the science behind life itself; it was mind-blowing.

Now, of course, these things are on popular science programmes on mainstream radio and TV, like *Horizon*, *The Life Scientific* or *The Infinite Monkey Cage*, but they are worth considering here because they have such a bearing on what happens to you when you meditate.

THE OBSERVER AFFECTS THE EXPERIMENT

Meditation is a trip into the recesses of your mind and consciousness and at the same time it is a tool to enable you to control your mind so that you can explore more and more effectively.

Science is now telling us that our awareness, our consciousness, influences the world around us.

Experiments have shown that just by focusing attention on something, we can subtly change it. For instance, we shall see that someone can affect the results of a random number generator in a laboratory even if the machine is in another town, so long as the person focuses on the machine.

It sounds crazy – but intriguing.

Please bear with me if physics is not a strong suit for you, I'm only trying to loosen our vice-like grip on what is possible and impossible.

The world is far more fluid and uncertain than we know with our senses, a fact that can disconcert and frighten us. When we are frightened, we contract, cling to what we think we know and shut out the rest. We have a tendency to deny the evidence in front of us because it doesn't fit in with our cherished paradigm of how the world works. We like to think that there is a dependable, clockwork order to it, and that we know the rules.

We think life is something that happens *to* us hapless victims. What if we have a hand in creating it ourselves?

According to Isaac Newton, I push my pen and it rolls until friction causes it to stop. I understand that. According to Descartes the world, including the human body, works like a machine, sort of clockwork. I understand that. But we are now told that in a bubble chamber down among the subatomic particles, there is no order at all. Particles actually come into and out of existence all the time. And time appears to go backwards as well as forwards.

We have ignored facts like this for about a hundred years, because they make no sense to us.

Let's try keeping an open mind, even try an experiment or two of our own before abandoning the whole thing.

What we are exploring is the power of our minds. And of course (here comes the meditation plug), a more powerful mind would be useful in so many ways.

THE DOUBLE SLIT EXPERIMENT

This famous experiment shows the effect of consciousness on matter. The 'double slit' experiment was performed by Thomas Young as far back as the early nineteenth century.

It is an experiment on the nature of light and how we affect it with our observations.

We notice that there are experiments that clearly show that light is a stream of tiny particles or photons. Evidence for this comes from the Compton effect, where electrons or photons are shown to recoil from exposure to x-rays as if they were billiard balls being hit by other billiard balls.

So everything is a particle.

Perfect.

Hold onto that thought, then imagine setting up Thomas Young's experiment:

We have a source of photon emissions, like a torch but emitting light one photon at a time, and in front of this 'torch' is a solid screen. The screen has two slits in it set off to either side of the centre. Beyond the screen is a light-sensitive plate. Now if a fine source of single colour light is directed at the screen and the photons are *particles* one would expect them to be absorbed into the screen in front of them, and not stand a cat in hell's chance of making it through the two side slits to get to the photo-sensitive plate behind. The photons would go straight into the screen, like bullets.

So far so good.

However, when the experiment is run, the light-sensitive plate at the back is changed, lines of interference appear on it, created by the photons. For this to happen the photons must have behaved like waves.

It is as if a wave fans out from the photon emitter and passes through the two slits at either side *at the same time*. The wave then becomes two smaller waves emerging one from each slit. The waves then spread out and intersect with each other and the peaks and troughs of one interfere with the peaks and troughs of the other producing the classic, striped, 'interference pattern' on the plate at the back, looking rather like a barcode.

Thus the double slit experiment shows very nicely thank you that light is a wave.

Yet surely, in our cause and effect world, this cannot be. A photon can't be both a particle and a wave.

But it is.

So it seems that if we set up an experiment to prove light is a particle, it's a particle, and if we set up an experiment to prove that light is a wave – it is a wave. So *we* affect the very nature of matter at this minute and basic level – the way we set up the experiment affects the outcome.

The observer affects the experiment.

There can no longer be a paradigm of absolute scientific method because the observer, no matter how scientific and rigorous she may be, affects the experiment.

No wonder Niels Bohr said that if we are not in awe of this stuff then we haven't understood it.

LET'S HEAR IT FOR SCHRODINGER

Science at the quantum level doesn't think of atoms as solid little balls. An atom of ice-cream is energy and is everywhere, but with the highest *probability* of it being in the ice-cream cone (and hopefully on your tongue before you can say 'physicist'.)

In what is known as the Copenhagen Interpretation, an atom, *when not observed*, spreads out through space according to an equation by Schrodinger. The equation apparently gives the chances of an atom being found in one location or another. Maybe there will be, say, a 20% probability of it being here and, say, an 80% probability of it being there.

Then, as soon as it is observed, it instantly plumps for one location or another – with 100% probability, this is called 'collapsing the probability wave'.

SCHRODINGER'S CAT

The physicist was driving his car and got pulled over by the police. The police checked everything, his papers, the mechanics of the car and the items in it. They opened the boot of the car, the officer straightened up and said, "Dr Schrodinger, there's a dead cat in your boot."

Schrodinger replied, "Well it is now."

I guess that physicists do have souls, and know that this is stuff is nuts.

To underline the craziness, Edwin Schrodinger imagined a cat sealed in a box with a vial of lethal poison which would be broken, and the poison released, depending on whether an unstable radioactive atom decayed or not. It had a 50% chance of decaying during the experiment, and so there was a 50% chance of poison being released into the air of the box, killing the cat. Quantum theory clearly allows for a state of both decay and non-decay at the same time (50% probability, of each) until an observation is made collapsing the probability into one state or the other,

The question Schrodinger posed was, until the box was opened and the cat observed, collapsing the probability, was the cat both alive and dead at the same time?

No unfortunate cat was harmed in this theoretical experiment. But it did show what a crazy world was being uncovered at the quantum level.

So what we see is determined by our seeing it. We collapse the probabilities. We, the observer, affect the very matter of our world; our awareness and our intentions, shape how it is.

We will see this even more convincingly when we apply it to our own intentions in a contemplation-meditation later. In this contemplation, you will see your intention, your mind, changing your own body energy, instantly, as it happens – live feedback.

But how could we all be changing stuff with our intentions without the world falling apart? Should we freak out, get frightened and stop investigating in case we intend something cataclysmic?

No, don't panic we are just finding out what actually happens all the time, we're not changing anything. We are not knocking any paradigms, not upsetting anyone else, just investigating our own experience.

And anyway, this knowledge has been out there for a hundred years since Einstein and Niels Bohr started the New Physics, and world has continued to turn. Our intentions are not focused enough to allow us to walk through a wall yet.

But there are countless experiments now, showing how our focused attention affects matter.

RANDOM NUMBER QUIRKINESS

Random numbers, can be generated by the decay of radioactive material. This should make the generation of the numbers immune from any attempted tampering by humans. That radioactive material will decay in its own random way, nothing to do with us.

Yet this decay *can* be affected by a volunteer focusing on a desired outcome.

If the output of our generator is either a zero or a one, by the law of averages there should be an equal number of zeros and ones coming out. But when the volunteer focuses on, say, more zeros, there are more zeros, or if the focus is on more ones, there are more ones. And the results obtained are way above chance.

This is called distant, non-local awareness and the data suggests it operates outside of space, hence non-local (because you don't have to be standing next to the generator), but also outside of time.

What?

Right, so the experiment works even if the subject is miles away from the generator, say in the next town. That's the non-local bit. Got that. But outside of time? How does that work?

This bit's tricky, deep breath:

The experiment will work if the generator's results have not been looked at (that would have collapsed the probabilities into concrete results) but are put in a sealed envelope as they come out of the machine. Then perhaps a month later, the subject focuses on a desired outcome *at the time of the run of the machine*, a month previously, intending say, more zeros or ones. The subject will still affect the results, as if he or she were doing it at the time of the number generation.

However, they will *not* be able to do it once someone has looked at the results. The act of looking, by anyone, will fix the results. But before that anything could happen, depending on the intention of the subject.

You're kidding me! Those results were printed on that paper a month before – can he/she change the printing? That's daft!

No, that's not what's happening, it's not that the focusing person affects the zeros and ones on the paper in the envelope when he is doing his focusing. The volunteer focuses his intention on a specific event, in this case the run of the numbers one month back, the machine *back then* is affected by his intention, as all probabilities are still up for grabs. The machine is affected by the focused intention a month in the future, and produces the intended results, *these* are then printed and sealed in the envelope.

Experiments like this were reviewed by William Braud, Director of the Institute of Transpersonal Psychology in Palo Alto, California, the odds against it happening by chance were 10,000 to 1.

Suffice it to say that we are left to wonder: if our intention, our consciousness, can do *this*, what *else* can it do? What are the ramifications of this? And is our consciousness more pivotal in the world as we see it than we could have dreamed? Does our intention shape our world?

The reason that it is worth considering is that if we affect the minute, subatomic particles, then we affect solid matter.

This is because there is in fact no such thing as solid matter. Everything is apparently mainly space. Our solid-looking matter is made of atoms. Atoms are just space and subatomic particles, these subatomic particles themselves are not solid, they are tiny specs, or vortices, of energy.

And as for the space, they say that if an atom were the size of the dome of St Paul's Cathedral the nucleus would be the size of an orange and the electrons the size of peas whizzing round it in the dome. So lots of space and a bit of swirling energy (or peas).

We are mainly space, and Marcus Chown says in his books, if we were able to suck all the space out of us, the whole human race would fit inside a sugar cube. Even stranger, the New Physics not only tells us that an electron or any other subatomic particle is not matter at all, it is just energy, but it's not even just energy, it is *potential for energy*.

This means that you can't pin it, or any quantum particle, down. If you know its location, you can't know its mass and if you know its mass you can't know its location (Heisenberg's Uncertainty Principle).

And an electron can even jump orbits within the atom *without ever being in the intervening space*, it just materialises in another orbit, just like the Tardis in *Doctor Who*.

So we, the daisies, the mountains and Heidi, are made of atoms which are just space and energy, or potential for energy.

These experiments show us that we can change matter. We will also be doing our own experiment in Chapters 15 and 16, observing our own energy system as it is changed by our intentions. Stay tuned!

6

A knock-your-socks-off
spiritual experience – the BKs

Along with the yoga, TM, and quantum weirdness, life had given me a wonderful second child, and postnatal depression (PND).

I was feeling emotionally as flat as a pancake with PND, and as I hadn't gone back to my job as a lawyer, maybe there was a touch of cabin-fever too. I heard that there was to be a festival of Mind Body and Spirit within easy driving distance of home.

There was a touch of opposition from my poor husband being left to cope with two tinies for a few hours, but, well, that was just too bad – did I mention my PND?

A two year old, a baby, jobs to do, feeling like shit – I was nice but firm. I'm going out.

I'd never been to a Mind Body and Spirit exhibition before. I might have been teaching yoga but I still had a highly developed critical faculty and could spot 'phony-holy-wanker' a mile off.

So there I was in this exhibition, and it was *huge*. I wandered dispiritedly (no pun intended) down rows of healers, crystal sellers and tarot readers. I saw a stall of stark white, with plump ladies in white saris and men in white trousers and white tops. It looked daft.

Looking at all that white kit I thought, 'You can take it all too far, you know,' and kept walking. I was so drained, absolutely nothing interested me and I wondered why I was there.

There was some dancing, rather amateurish and earnest, being performed by a group in the middle of the hall who were also wearing white. One bloke in particular was staring unwaveringly at me, I stared right back thinking, 'Yeah, yeah, and we all know what you want!'

OK, it doesn't sound too spiritual, but I was a lawyer for Pete's sake, cynicism comes with the territory.

I was prepared to reduce it all to the lowest common denominator: the Hall was making money from the stall-holders, the stall-holders were making money out of the punters, and all men wanted sex. That nailed it for me. I was a young, unaccompanied woman, so why not hit on me?

How wrong could I be (this happens to me a lot – being wrong, I mean)? The group were all Bramha Kumaris and he was probably celibate and was staring, not into my eyes, but at my third eye in my forehead, between and just above my eyebrows.

I watched the dance, critically, then turned away and wandered back to the stalls intending to do another circuit and go home. When I came to the isle with the very white stall I just went marching into to it. Don't ask me why.

They were the Bramha Kumaris, it turns out. I was so drawn to the girl who talked to me that I agreed to go to their centre in Leeds to learn more.

In the end I did a course with them. There was a bit to swallow though, stuff about time being cyclic and the different ages within the cycle, and that this was a special time, before the cycle started again. Yeah, right.

They also said that the soul resided in-between the eyebrows and was an infinitely small dot, and that God was an infinitely small dot residing in the soul world.

What? Where?

Was all this strictly necessary?

It didn't resonate with me, I felt that truth had to be more simple than this. But I did like the idea of the power source being infinite, whether that be infinitely small or infinitely large, somehow those concepts seemed the same. Infinity was infinity. And whatever power made all this work had to be infinite.

So I could cope with God being a small dot. And the thing was that you could simply focus on that God dot and it was lovely.

In a meditation session, the Bramha Kumaris person conducting it would sit at the front and focus on God in the soul world, like a star. The power of this dot or star came down, like light, into the dot in the forehead of the BK. That BK would then look at you, at the dot between your eyebrows, and then would allow the energy streaming into her to stream into you. So she would channel God energy into you.

It all sounded far-fetched, except that it *worked*. It was incredibly powerful.

This infinite energy that was God was deemed to have the qualities of love, peace, purity, knowledge and wisdom, and you could consider these as you contemplated the God dot. But whatever you might or might not be thinking about it still worked.

A friend and I used to go to the BKs together and we were both sceptical about the bigger story about cyclic time and stuff, and we used to get the giggles and say what if they were right? What if we died and discovered that was how it was? We'd feel a bit silly then.

Anyway one day we took my friend's sister-in-law with us and were so busy chatting in the car on the way there that we forgot to tell Lucy (not her name, but I think it might suit her) what would happen.

Sitting there cross-legged on the floor with all these people in white, the men on one side and women on the other side of an aisle, with a bloke at the front meditating and looking holy I thought, what the ---- is Lucy going to make of this?

Back in the car on the way home Lucy is bursting with it. "When he looks at you, that bloke at the front! When he looks at you, you can feel this thing," she paused, "here!" She pointed to her third eye.

DYNAMIC DIWALI

Soon it was Diwali and we were back, sitting in serried ranks on the floor. The place was packed. My head was on a swizzle stick looking at all the beautiful saris of the visiting Indian ladies. I was looking backwards towards the door when I felt this amazing power filling my head and chest. 'Gosh, it's is starting early,' I thought, then turned round to find a bloke had come in and sat down at the front and was focusing on me. It was astonishing. I wasn't even thinking about the meditation at that point, just admiring the beautiful saris.

I still do the BK practice sometimes and it provides an instant lift. A spiritual shot in the arm. The lovely thing is that you can contact and focus on this energy for yourself, without anyone leading you, and we will.

I certainly went for it full tilt at the time, I had never experienced power like it. It changed me, together with a visit to a homeopath, from being utterly miserable to being full of love and smiles for the world. It was a game changer.

It marked the beginning of a developing spiritual awareness. As it was a form of devotion and so delightful, it was easy to surrender into it. It wasn't an intellectual thing, it was a gorgeous experience and I found that my concentration increased effortlessly. Who wouldn't concentrate when it's all so lovely?

MY KUNDALINI TRIP

There were some important BKs coming from India. (Important? You see that rankled with me – how can there be hierarchies in the spirit? You get my drift?) There was to be a big meditation meeting in a hall somewhere and the kids and I spent the afternoon putting out chairs in rows for people. I went home and gave the children tea, baths and bedtime stories and nearly didn't bother to go back for the meditation. But I did…

Then an extraordinary thing happened. After the meditation we all formed a line and went up to receive gifts of food from the visiting big-wigs, it's what they always did. Wanting to get off home, I was wondering about the time as I shuffled forward in the line.

This Indian man put an apple in my hand and looked at me. At that moment there was this massive whoosh of energy from the base of my spine up to my head and out of the top. It was astonishing, the physical sensation of something racing up through me and out of the top of my head like an out-of-control elevator.

I was in shock. I looked back to the man, dazed and probably with my mouth open. He was giving an apple to someone else.

That was it.

I was sidestepping along the line of dignitaries, receiving a piece of cake this time – and in need of counselling!

THE NUTS AND BOLTS

This was inherently empowering, but I did also put in a lot of work. I got up at 4am and meditated for two hours, I meditated for an hour at lunchtime and an hour at night as well as five minutes every couple of hours. This was organised around my domestic routine because I was at home and my kids were tiny. It certainly helped me cope with the tedium of washing, cooking, shopping – it all became easy, a joy. It was as if this dot of God was in my life. I (silently!) spoke to him all the time calling him Baba (Daddy), I shared everything that happened to me, everything I saw, with him. God was my imaginary friend.

It sounds mad, but I did this for quite a few years and became more and more powerful, though not a Bramha Kumaris.

Something was certainly happening, but I wasn't sure what. I thought it was something to do with the practice of surrender into the *concept* of God, a higher power, and I didn't see the need to join and take on board the whole story. I had a few skirmishes but couldn't accept it, and hated any idea of cults or brainwashing.

They were fine with that and I became a sort of honorary BK for a while until something else happened to rock my world. But before we get on to that, let's have a go at the meditation I'm talking about.

MEDITATION ON GOD AS A DOT

Sitting quietly as before. Take a few deep breaths to relax your shoulders and allow your focus on the breath to bring you into this moment.

As you come into the present, focus on the idea of there being an infinitely small dot, imagine it as a distant star, beaming light down to you. You experience the light from the star in your third eye, between your eyebrows where you reside as a tiny dot also.

Feel the beauty and fortuitousness of being bathed in the golden light from the star. Feel it focusing and collecting in your third eye. Enjoy the sensation of slight warmth and wellbeing.

Feel the love in that light, allow the love to reach you, expanding you. Feel the love in your third eye and allow yourself to soften and surrender into this inpouring of love. Allow it to spread, filling your head, your body. You become enveloped in light and love. Enjoy it. God is infinite love, there is no end to this love. There is only limitless, boundless, ineffable love.

This love cannot hurt you.

Enjoy the feeling, surrender utterly. What have you got to lose? Trying to be constantly vigilant and in control hasn't done it for you, so try surrender. Become the child in the infinite embrace of the Father/Mother. As the dot that is you surrenders into the infinite dot of love it fills you, you are floating, free, expanded, you are the Universe, totally loved.

Total love.

Then consider the light as purity. God is purity, there is no agenda there. This dot of love is not trying to manipulate you or get you on Its side. It is not adapting Itself to suit, It's just as It is, pure. It just is.

This is so safe, It is purity and pure love. It feels dependable, safe, true. You feel your armour melting.

Nothing is going to hurt you, you can start to relax, to allow love in. This purity allows the love space in you to flourish.

Within this cocoon of love and purity consider *knowledge*. God is all knowledge. He knows all the bits of you. Yes, and that bit too! Oh no!

He knows what we perceive as the 'bad' bits in the whole of creation and yet He loves. Total knowledge – and with this intimate and all-embracing knowledge, of what and why and how it is, there is no judgement, only love. All is as it should be, perfection, love. Allow a sense of gratitude to arise. A feeling of wonder that compassion is so all encompassing.

Then there is absolute wisdom. With infinite knowledge there comes infinite wisdom. He knows all and He understands. She knows how it is, She knows why it is and She loves. God is everything, past, present and future. God is beyond time and space, He is all of it, now. And His wisdom is infinite. Being all of it, She is utterly wise. There is no way to pull the wool over her eyes, nowhere to hide, there is always God and there is always love. She knows, and yet She understands and loves.

Become aware of the peace in this light. Consider the infinite quality of peace. Allow yourself to flow into absolute peace. This is peace, not just for Christmas, it's peace that goes on forever.

Endless now, endless peace.

You can expand forever into this peace. Expanding endlessly in seamless calm and serenity – it feels so good.

Bathing in the glow of God. That distant star of light.

Absolute love.

Absolute purity.

All knowledge.

Complete wisdom.

Absolute peace.

Allow yourself to be held in the light of God, feel that light coming into your third eye. Dissolve in endless and all-encompassing love. Become all of the qualities of love, purity, knowledge, wisdom and peace as you merge in surrender to the infinity of the dot.

Smiling in gratitude, give thanks for the love and return to the room.

~

People say great things after a BK meditation; one Californian man turned to me a said: "I just got Blaasted!"

If I have been over-liberal in the use of the G word, I'm sorry, but it's an integral part of the BK surrendering, as they tell it. You could substitute *qi* or energy and it would work just as well.

However the idea of a God does need to be explored, is it necessary, and what is it? And does He wear a long white frock?

7

God, the Beard,
the Cloud, the Smiting

I always had trouble with God.

As a protestant brought up in a Roman Catholic convent school I'd been put right off. The nuns were not a happy bunch, possibly going into the convent for strong emotional or family reasons years ago, and repenting at leisure, who knows? But they certainly made our lives grim. They didn't seem to like us much.

If that was what God was all about, I didn't want to know.

It took me a long time to realise that, apart from the teeth-gritting experience of the convent, my gripe with Christianity was mainly to do with Rome taking over and skewing the whole thing with the weapon of guilt, for power purposes.

I largely ignored the wonder of Christ (who is love, and utterly gorgeous, as love always is).

And even when I was able to see all that, I was *still* pretty anti. Then, of course, God got thrown out with the bathwater.

I knew there was *something*, some all-encompassing something, some power out there. I mean, I couldn't make a snowdrop or cows' noses. There had to be something making it all work, or at least something that started it all off.

I noticed that I could accept the idea of a *power* 'out there', but was not comfortable with the *personification* of God. The idea of giving the Force that infuses and encompasses the Universe: black holes and a supernova right down to a soil bacterium or a complex 11-week-old foetus – that Force – the idea of giving it a personality, was impossible. It didn't add up.

Because then you get the capricious God, who is pleased with your sacrifice, whom you must not *dis*please or he'll smite you – that's the angry God who destroys a city and so on.

And in Its personification, God becomes property that you can possess, appease and align with. It becomes, or rather *He* becomes, *my* God. And guess what, my God is better than your God and then, bam, we have another excuse for war. Good to put that testosterone to use and with God on our side, it's a no-brainer, off we go.

LOVE AND FEAR

This cross, partisan God bore no relation to the soft but glorious ineffability I felt when I meditated. I couldn't accept it.

My experience told me that what I awoke to in meditation was incredible power, yes, but also the most earth-shattering love and compassion. There was no room for the negative. It was the sort of love that took your breath away and lifted and expanded you until you were all possibilities – does that make sense?

I had also come to the conclusion that there is only fear or love.

Anger and all things negative come from fear.

The rest is love.

Love is what I experienced as God-stuff, the Matrix of it all. (It gets tricky when you don't use the G word, so from now on, if I use the G word can we take it I mean this Universal Force, the Field, Source, the Oneness, whatever…?) It's the power that makes it all work and It feels wonderful.

So that's love.

What about the fear?

Fear comes from believing that you are *not* the Oneness.

If you are not the Oneness, then you must be a tiny, separate you – in a great big universe. The fear is the fear that you are alone and *weak*, your survival is in question. You have to be vigilant, responding to aggression, or attacking first from fear of possible aggression.

This aloneness gives you the fear that you will not have enough, so you have to take. And you need more. You need more for now and even more for later. In fact, you just do what you have to do to survive in a dangerous place, you covet, you lie, you steal.

That human part of us is desperate to survive. And I'd love to think that this doesn't include lovely us! That if there was one piece of bread between us on the table and we were both starving we would be saying, 'No *you* must have it'. But who knows?

Yet I noticed that in the state of love that comes with meditation there *is* no fear. All needs are met and anyway the love that permeates me, and *is* me, is in and about everything so nothing is 'other'. We are all one. There is nothing to fight about and nobody with whom to fight.

AM I ALONE IN THINKING THIS?

I read about Taoism and the *Tao Te Ching*, the ancient writings of Lao Tzu, supposedly an old man in China who was going home to die but who wrote down his wisdom first.

I loved it, it was talking my language, a language of inclusion not exclusion.

The Tao is described as the Way, the way of things, the flow of life, and also the force that is in all life. Naturally I felt drawn to the idea of a force that permeates all things, a ground force out of which all things spring. That fitted with my experience.

It also fitted with the idea in quantum mechanics of a quantum field, energy, force, where what we call reality is only an endless series of interactions within that field (affected by mind).

As far as I could see everything was energy, organised by consciousness.

It would seem that reality was far more strange than anything we could make up. Yet we appeared to *be* making things up, the world seemed so real and yet was smoke and mirrors.

Nothing had substance, nothing was real – and yet, paradoxically, pinch me and it hurts.

AND WHAT ABOUT GOD?

There was no denying, for me, that the BK meditation was tremendously powerful, but why did there need to be a God involved with a story of his own, a different storyline to the Christian God or to the pantheon of Hindu gods?

All these religions were ways in, but they all seemed to be a bit insane, each in its own way, and to involve very specific vocabularies, clothing and insufficient humour.

A friend suggested that I go to a retreat in the South of France with an ex-hippie called Ram Dass. The friend knew I had a low tolerance for the pious or the phony-holy, but he assured me that Ram Dass was a teacher's teacher and spot on.

Sure enough, in a crumbling chateau in France I discovered lots of remarkable, sane, funny and delightful people listening to wonderfully sane, funny and delightful Ram Dass telling it like it is; how life is, and how it works.

I would still get up early and go to the big hall to meditate in peace and spaciousness at 5am, and then be happy to do Tai Chi and chanting before breakfast with the others followed by a lecture from RD – it was brilliant.

THE BREAKTHROUGH

Then one day RD taught us how to do Buddhist Vipassana meditation.

Sitting on my pillow roll at the back of the hall, the instruction was to focus your attention on the breath at the end of the nose, just watching it come in and go out, or to watch the rising and falling of the abdomen with each breath.

He pointed out that the mind would try to distract us, there would be thoughts and sensations. When we noticed the thought we should acknowledge thinking and return to the breath. As far as sensations were concerned, we might get an itch, or a pain in the shoulder, say. The art was not to scratch the itch or move the shoulder if one could help it. Just acknowledge the sensation and return to the breath.

That was the instruction, simply watch: acknowledge sensation, or thinking, and return to the breath. 'OK! Bring it on,' I thought, I was, after all, a meditator. (This is sheer hubris – you know I'm going to come a cropper, don't you!)

There I was at the back of the huge hall, sitting comfortably on my cushion. The breath, I could do this. Easy.

A few thoughts, I sank back into the breath.

Then there was *the* most excruciating pain in my knee – I mean agony. I had to move my knee or it would be irreparably damaged. Then the thought: 'What the …? I'm a *meditator*, I'm used to sitting cross-legged, what's this about?'

'Aha, this is the ego, trying to distract me. RD said this would happen.' I so wanted to move, but this was Buddhist meditation, full of rigor, I would really try.

OK, go back to the breath, it still hurt, notice the pain, acknowledge it, back to the breath.

After a few trips to the pain and back to the breath, suddenly I was *above my body*, free and blissful. The pain was going on but it was 'down there' in the body, and of no concern to me.

Then I got it, like a bombshell.

This is who we are.

This transcendent being, this love and bliss, this is reality. I was having direct experience of who I was.

So, what can I learn from this? If you get out of your own way, underneath your complicated, constructed life, you are *all* of it. You always were all of it. What an insight, I felt liberated from the tyranny of *belief* systems into the freedom of bald *experience*.

All you have to do is surrender who you think you are, your ego, into something else, in this case the breath. You surrender in order to get out of the way of the ego and who you thought you were, with the your fascinating story. And bingo, there it was, an entirely altered state of consciousness. Interesting.

BYE-BYE BELIEF

I got it. I didn't have to *believe* in a god or someone's version of events that made me feel uncomfortable. This power, these altered and glorious states of consciousness were here all along, the subtext to existence. Sure, you could get the awareness of them through belief in a god, if that was your thing, but you didn't have to go that way. There was a simpler truth than that.

Although the religious practices themselves can be fabulous and wonderful practices and signposts on the way, all practices lead to this.

I was the Force (as are we all), or part of it, but I hadn't known it because I was so absorbed in my mundane life. By channelling my thinking into the tiny movement of the breath (or the tiny dot of the BKs, or the concept of any other god presumably) who I truly was could be revealed.

It's the surrender that does it.

This is who we are. This is what is real when we stop making up stories.

We just need to get out of the way. Lure the thinking mind away, down a safe cul-de-sac, like the boring old breath, surrendering utterly into that. Then...

This is real.

This is what we glimpse spontaneously a few times in a lifetime if we are lucky. This is what we experience watching that sunset or when we lose ourselves fishing, knitting or whatever!

Only we don't have to have the sunset or fishing rod. We just need to surrender into the moment utterly and experience the full-on glory of what we really are.

This is leading us towards the Buddhist practice of Vipassana, concentration on the breath.

The simplest thing to surrender into is always going to be the breath, it's here as long as we are. Also there is no belief system, which is useful if belief makes you feel uncomfortable, or it can fit right in if you do have a belief.

It's only your breath, you can do this.

8

What about Vipassana, insight meditation?

Vipassana meditation is basically following the breath; it doesn't sound too promising, I have to admit. But then, that's what is so brilliant about it too. It's simple.

VIPASSANA AND MINDFULNESS – ARE THEY THE SAME?

Vipassana and Mindfulness are both meditations on the breath. Here I will describe Vipassana as practiced in Southern Buddhism and we will have a go at doing it in the next chapter, you will see the similarities to Mindfulness.

Mindfulness is very popular because it works. It does what it says it will do, it helps you reduce stress and live a life. It has a more open and inclusive focus than Vipassana and requires less concentration. It's relatively easy, and it gets a great press.

But we need a focused mind. Vipassana is about training the mind, developing *focus* and *concentration*, always simply bringing the mind back to the breath when you find you are on a mental trip to Disney World, rather than examining the thoughts of Mickey and Minnie and any attendant feelings that have taken you away from the breath.

You will quiet down and become more peaceful, as you would in Mindfulness. But more than this, you are honing your consciousness to be a one-pointed tool for cutting through illusion, which is of terrific value in your quest for ultimate truth.

With no frills, Vipassana is straightforward, you can see clearly how it all works and you gain insight. It's the light-sabre of meditation.

Also, within the practice of Mindfulness, you can be mindful only to the extent that you can keep your mind on the present moment (duh!), so increasing your concentration is incredibly useful.

Am I selling it to you?

VIPASSANA/INSIGHT

All you do is follow the breath.

As you sit there with your mind confined to the breath, you notice a procession of trivial, rubbishy thoughts. You simply acknowledge the thought, paying attention to it (not suppressing it), then let it go and return to the breath.

Maybe the thought is about unfinished business, or times when you have behaved badly. The things that make you go hot when you think about them: 'Oh God, did I say that?' or 'I didn't do *that*, did I?' It all trots out before your inner gaze as you sit. And it's hell. The detritus, and the pointlessness of your life, it's awful, but it's real. That's your life. What a nasty shock.

You get such insight into *you*, your daydreams and your mellow drama. Because of course, you can't run away, switch on the TV or phone a friend. You're especially stuck if you are on a retreat or meditating with others; you just sit, stewing.

But pennies drop. You see what makes you feel good and what makes you feel bad.

The nasty side of you, the spiteful, aggressive bits that pop up feel like dog-doo. And if any good bits make the cut, they feel gorgeous.

Well, it doesn't take an Einstein to work out your optimal course for the future does it? Be aggressive and bad-tempered and it will feel rubbish inside. Be kind and loving and it will be harmonious, you will be able to live easy with yourself. Good insight.

Right, so Vipassana is insight meditation. Seeing how it is.

Why use the breath?

As you focus on the breath, you notice that it goes in and out, in and out... boring. You could notice that it is warm or cold, moist or dry, but then you run out of attributes.

The thing is though, the breath is always with you, so it's handy, and it is moving just a smidge so it gives your mind a tiny bit to do, which is also quite handy. And of course the breath is in the moment, in the here and now, so focusing on it brings *you* into the here and now. Mega-handy.

I CAN'T MEDITATE – I THINK ALL THE TIME

At first the mind is all over the place and at this point people usually give up, saying they just can't meditate. Well, the mind is only doing what it has always done, dodging about here and there, unchecked. You simply never noticed before.

We all assume that we are in control of the mind but it only takes ten minutes of following the breath to knock that one on the head. Or perhaps it would be better to say 45 minutes of following the breath – in a lesser time you might indeed think it was easy. But then the quicksilver mind slips away and it's having the same row with your sister that it's had a million times. And you notice, eventually.

So why does the mind do this?

Easy, it is protecting your ego, your constructed self. You spend so much, in fact nearly all, of your energy creating and bolstering this artificial you, the ego construct. If you allow the mind the astonishing experience of nothing but bare focus, there is no *story*, so there is nothing for the ego to get its teeth into.

The real problem for the ego is that the final destination of meditation is enlightenment, the merging back into the Oneness, the experience that there is no difference between the Oneness and you, and me and everything. At one level, there's only one of us here, and it's not the paltry little ego invented by you this lifetime.

Enlightenment is the ultimate disappointment for the ego. None of your drama would be of interest to you in an enlightened state. All would be God, One, the Oneness. It is the death of the individual you, the separate self, the ego construct.

The ego will throw up any smokescreen to stop you meditating to avoid this fate.

Strange as it may seem, the ego is, after all, nothing but the sum of the story of your life, created by the mind, up to this point. The ego was, amazingly, constructed by you, out of all the things that have happened to you, and have conditioned you to think the way you do.

You made it up. It's your story and it's who you think you are. And in meditation we are allowing the story to quiet down, by being in the moment with the breath.

No story! Oh, bloody hell! And of course ultimately, in this or some other lifetime, we *will* go beyond the limits of the ego story and become enlightened.

Well no wonder the ego goes nuts. The mind is yelling: 'Hey, I'm a thought, think me!' There is a monologue: 'Remember when I… nobody likes me because… I look silly and all my friends will laugh… I don't have any friends, not really… I can go and get a pizza after this… in fact I could get up right now… this is a waste of my time.'

The common denominator in all the stories is 'I, me, mine'.

If you have a *stormy* story, a hot conflict, you are immersed in the drama of being you, and thus the ego exists. You might die in the conflict but the ego will go down with the ship. If there is just the breath, where is the storyline? Where is the all-absorbing, endless thinking and conflict?

HUMAN AND DIVINE

Lest this all seem too depressing, pointless with the gas oven beckoning, the joy is that once you 'get it', you can really enjoy your life. There is this moment, and in this moment there is joy, it's official.

It's the beautiful paradox of being totally human and existing whether you like it or not (we did incarnate after all) and yet being all the rest of it at the same time.

Ram Dass called it 'vertical schizophrenia'. That means that you are a body, a personality type, a particular sexuality, a specific ethnicity, an archetype (bagsey I be the hero), and so on until you get to being the Oneness, as well.

You are all of it.

All at once

Right now.

So you can't lose yourself in any one of them. Not in holiness – the baby needs a new pair of shoes – and not in lust and grunting, at least not forever (nice try though).

We are all of it and as we quiet down we become gloriously aware of that.

Mostly though, we are usually very aware of the bodily states and our drama, and less aware of our more spiritual states. Yet they are all here, when we are in the moment.

That's where meditation and Vipassana come in, you just follow the breath and it all happens.

The more focused you become on the breath, the more the storyline drops away, it is not being reinforced by constant thoughts, and there is only the breath. The breath becomes your haven from thoughts and their resulting emotions, and ultimately you merge with the breath. Then another reality shows up, a reality of spaciousness and peace. It was behind the thoughts all the time. You have been looking for this peace and acceptance all your life, only you never knew it was available, waiting for you to open to it.

I know we're talking the Oneness again – all methods lead through to this. This merging back into the Oneness is enlightenment. But there is usually a lot of meditation to be done before that happens. The good news is that getting there is wonderful, with all these great, altered states of consciousness to experience, you'll love it.

Then, ta da, there is a space beyond even these high, refined states where suddenly: *It just is*, and you are not.

So first you are there, experiencing astonishing states of consciousness beyond the mundane work-a-day world. Then wham, suddenly there is no being there, nobody experiencing. It just is – and you are nowhere. It is direct knowing, direct experience (don't worry, this is definitely the advanced course!)

Well the individual, 'me, me, me' ego is not going to like that one bit. That's why it seems so hard at first with all the thoughts getting in the way. But the ego also flings up physical stuff too.

SENSATIONS

So here you are, focusing on the breath and your thoughts are playing out past and future fantasies incessantly. You have what is called monkey-mind. You keep acknowledging, letting go and returning to the breath.

You might just be getting the upper hand and start feeling a bit peaceful with fewer thoughts and then – there's a huge pain.

It can't be the ego, you can't believe it, this pain is so real.

Focusing back on the breath the pain may move somewhere else. If the pain remains you can focus on that and then return to the breath. Go to the pain back to the breath. Open to the pain, back to the breath.

If the pain gets unbearable, you may decide to move, but do it consciously.

I mean how many times do you have an itch and scratch it without even raising a thought? That scratching is just automatic, completely unconscious, you are on autopilot. But here we are trying to be super-aware, conscious. The Buddha was the awakened one, after all.

Talking of itches, when I first started doing this stuff I used to take a little vow at the beginning of the session that I wouldn't move until the end. Well, the *itches!* I used to get a bit of dust or something alighting on my cheek and *pow*, it felt like Vesuvius erupting. It was huge, this sensation of irritation, of explosive itchiness, it was more than flesh and blood could stand.

Now it is so interesting, and of course, such an insight, that if you do nothing about the pain, the itch, the annoying sound, whatever it is, and just acknowledge sensation (even sound is sensation – of sound waves on your ear drum) and go back to the breath, then... after doing this a few times, suddenly your *foot* hurts, or a different bit of you itches.

Then you get it: it was never real anyway. It was always just another story made up by the mind to stop you meditating. The death of the ego? Remember, the ego goes down fighting, it doesn't like it and it's clever.

SPACIOUSNESS

Transcending the mundane and being in spaciousness itself is what you were born to do. In fact you have been spaciousness all along, you just didn't know it.

There was always that nagging question. What's it all for, this life business? What *is* the point? It ends in death you know!

I mean, you know where your present way of thinking and distractions will lead – another TV programme, another shopping trip, another love affair, whatever. And it's all the same stuff – like a long-running soap opera. There is a fundamental lack of satisfaction in the material world. Nothing stays the same, nothing's quite enough, you always want more. You are left with the lament: 'Is that all there is?'

No, clearly not.

Don't go away.

First though, are there other ways out of the problem, other ways to transcend the lack of satisfaction, the frustrations? Well, drugs have an obvious appeal because they take you out of your mundane, cause-and-effect, universe. But their effect is temporary, you can't stay there, and anyway they are bad for you and illegal.

Romantic love provides a joyous escape, but it's just lust in a suit with a rose between its teeth. It's a good diversion, providing a great numbing of the critical faculty, but unfortunately it doesn't answer the BIG question, it just postpones it. And it doesn't last either – usually only long enough to ensure procreation and the survival of the species. Harsh I know, but depressingly true.

So is there any way to escape into a higher and more meaningful consciousness, to give some form or perspective to our lives? Yes, plenty of ways, and they are all paths going to the same place or state. However, the great thing about *this* path, following the breath, is that it has no storyline, no belief system, and it is all the more amazing for that.

BACK TO MY STORY, ME, ME, ME

To recap: all the times I had done the lovely Brahma Kumaris meditations, surrendering into a deity story, I would go into the most wonderful bliss states. But I didn't buy the whole BK package, lovely though it was.

Then I did Vipassana with Ram Das and I was in absolute bliss and not connected to my body.

So hold on, I was in bliss, having an out-of-body experience, and it was without any focus on a God figure, without the uncomfortable leap of faith into someone else's story. Just focusing on the breath, nothing else and there it was, bliss.

That was, as I have said, my eureka moment. Total surrender of who I thought I was and – incredible bliss.

So impressive.

I was such a happy meditator on that retreat. I had the wonderful stories of Ram Dass, the incredible spiritual chants of Jai Lakshman and I had the simplicity and purity of the breath taking me to absolute peace and endless bliss (via exploding itches on the cheek and excruciating, disappearing knee pains of course.)

At the time, I had hair that was spikey on top, gelled up like blasted rain forest stumps (trust me is was a great look at the time and very easy to 'do' on a retreat. A girl has to think of these things).

One early morning I had been practicing tai chi on the terrace with lots of people and it was lovely. We trooped in through the French doors, with trailing greenery cascading down from above the door frame, to do our early morning meditation. All very wonderful. Big mats were pushed together so the huge hall was a sea of mats with our bed pillow rolls put down to sit on.

I took my place, the gong went and I went into deep meditation, it was a wonderful peaceful space.

Then there was a movement in my hair.

I imagined a spider had landed on my head as I came through the doors. Somehow I was not concerned. I would be still. It would be peaceful. Back to the breath.

Movement. Maybe I was moving a little, disturbing it? Back to the breath. Bliss, delight.

At the end of the 45-minute session the gong went, we stretched our fingers, I bowed, bending down, still cross-legged, lowering my head towards the floor and a large white scorpion dropped onto the mat in front of me and scuttled down between the mats.

It all felt so surreal and yet perfectly normal.

We went into breakfast.

I use this story to illustrate the fact that simply following the breath in this narrow, focused way can take you to some pretty amazing places and is not to be sneezed at. It turns out that the bliss state is just for starters. It is what is known as the first jhana, or altered state of consciousness, though I didn't know that at the time.

I did go spontaneously into the jhanas on another occasion and will talk about it later – but for now, just to experience the bliss was extraordinary enough.

~

My daughter was drawn to meditation when on a gap year in Thailand. She eventually took the robes and became a Buddhist nun for a year in her Thai monastery. She wrote to me one time, commenting that all her life I had told her she had no need to take drugs because if she meditated she could go to the same places as drugs would take her. She had assumed that I meant she would feel peaceful and see the futility of getting continually, and temporarily, high.

"However," she said, "you didn't mean that at all, I have just experienced

BLISS!

Just think," she added, "you've been a bliss queen all these years and I never knew."

You see, it's not just me, it *is* good.

9

Let's do Vipassana.
How hard can it be?

This is not complicated, we all have breath.
We know that Vipassana means insight.
Insight happens, when you are awake.
Our method is simply to follow the breath,
awake and aware. You can do this. I promise.

PREPARATION

Choose a peaceful place, you may want to keep a room or corner of a room for meditation purposes, it can help you focus if it is familiar and you could possibly build up good vibes there.

You need to be comfortable, maybe having a blanket or throw around your shoulders so as not to feel chilled. Then, you could do without being disturbed, perhaps letting others in the house know that you are having a quiet time.

Decide how long your meditation session will be and stick to it. Have a clock nearby that you can see easily, or even a timer – I recommend a subtle one, rather than one with a catastrophically loud pinging noise, could give you a nasty shock at the end, especially if you aren't particularly awake and aware at that point.

The reason for the clock or timer is so that you don't have to get up to go and see what the time is, nobody goes back again, even if only five minutes have gone by. And the point about sticking to the time allotted is that we are trying, ever so gently, to control our minds, possibly for the first time ever. And the mind will give you incredibly plausible reasons why you have to abandon this meditation session immediately. It is astonishing how inventive your mind can be. You just have to get up, now, it's imperative. Then once you're up you can see that the reason was just hype and not important at all.

THE POSTURE

Sit comfortably, cross-legged on a cushion on the floor, or sit on a chair with your feet firmly planted on the floor. Have your back straight, and if on a chair, have your back a little away from the back of the chair, this helps with the flow of *qi* but also, if you slouch you are more likely to nod off.

Have the hands palms down or up on the thighs, or loosely placed in the lap, one on top of the other. Don't fold the arms or lace fingers, both are too defensive. The idea behind the posture is to be *stable*, so that you are comfortable and not going to fall over; *relaxed*, in a position that is easy to maintain; and *open*, notice that sitting in a chair with your arms crossed and your legs entwined feels closed – and we're trying to put our armour down and be open to what is.

Lower the chin slightly so as to create the feeling of space between the back of the head, the occiput, and the neck. This area can get so tense that the Taoists train you to create space and relaxation here to allow *qi* to flow. No matter how relaxed you feel you can always relax this area some more. There is an acupuncture point just below the occiput, and it is stimulated if you gently rub just here as you settle down to meditate. Some people find this helpful.

Having established a stable and comfortable position, settle in, feel at home on your cushion, be comforted by the Buddhist belief that much merit is attained by simply sitting down to meditate. It is given to very few to take this path, they say – so how brill are you?

NOW RELAX

To relax you initially, take a few deep breaths.

For the first breath hunch your shoulders up to your ears as you breathe in and relax the shoulders down on the out-breath.

It is easier to relax on the out-breath.

You can then breathe in through the nose with a longer out-breath through the mouth for a few breathing rounds, inviting relaxation with each exhalation.

Then breathe normally in and out through the nose.

The breath helps you to feel alert and relaxed.

Be aware of where you are, your surroundings. Close the eyes gently. Be aware of the noises in the room, in the street outside. Let these noises be, they do not need to disturb you now.

Allow the scents and sounds of the room to become a loving backdrop for your exploration within, rather than an irritation which has to be dealt with or ignored. Just accept.

Smile, and allow the sunshine of your smile to soak through your body, making you feel good. Why not? Enjoy your own endorphin production.

To begin:

LIGHTHOUSE/LOVING-KINDNESS MEDITATION

It is common in Buddhist practice to do a loving-kindness meditation at the beginning of the session. The more love you give, the more your love grows.

With your eyes lightly closed imagine that you are beaming out loving-kindness in a beautiful golden light to the front of you, like a lighthouse. The huge, broad beam of light encompasses all beings in front of you, with no exceptions.

May all beings be happy, may all beings be free from suffering.

Allow your beam to go out to *every* being in front of you, including your business partner, your mother-in-law, the man who cut you up in the car. All beings. Stretching out to infinity, through the walls, through all obstacles, beyond the limits of the earth, out into space and on and on.

Then send your light to the right of you, again with no exceptions.

May all beings be happy, may all beings be free from suffering.

Then behind you. A big broad beam of golden light. Stretching out to infinity.

May all beings be happy, may all beings be free from suffering.

Then to the left of you:

May all beings be happy, may all beings be free from suffering.

Then above you, send your magnificent beam of love, out to infinity, encompassing all possible worlds and beings. On and on for ever.

May all beings be happy, may all beings be free from suffering.

Now below you, through the earth, including all the creatures in the earth below you, all beings on the planet on the other side of the earth with no exceptions and on, out to infinity.

May all beings be happy, may all beings be free from suffering.

And for yourself, and observe any resistance to the thought:

May I be happy, may I be free from suffering.

Feel it.

Rest for a moment in the space of love that you have created. Absorb the love and wellbeing and realise that you have created this within you, with your intention and focus on loving kindness. Notice that it feels good.

Be aware that if you can't wish happiness and freedom from suffering for yourself it is just, in a strange way, ego. You are saying that you, in particular, are unworthy. That means that all other beings in the Universe are worthy of receiving this light of love and compassion, but not you. You are the perfect one who has not made the cut, who has failed in some way and is therefore unworthy. More was expected of you that any other being, clearly.

No. Let's get real. Welcome to the human race. You are just as fallible, just as rubbishy and just as worthy of limitless love as the rest of us.

MEDITATION ON THE BREATH

As you sit, become aware of the breath. Watch the breath as if you were a sentry sitting at the end of the nose. See the breath come in and go out. You are not following the breath into the body, giving you scope to wonder at the miracle of lungs, trying to remember what alveoli were all about and who it was who taught you biology at school. Nor are you following the breath out into the room, into the world, into the lungs of others, the person next to you, an aged rock star on another continent. All that gives too many story opportunities for the mind.

Just observing the breath at the nostrils. You can watch the breath coming in and going out, cool or warm, moist or dry, that's about it. Just the breath. You are giving your mind something to do, but not a lot.

Let your focus be light, not heavy-duty concentration. Just the breath, that's all.

If you find the breath at the nostrils too difficult for any reason, then focus on the belly, the rising and falling of the abdomen with each breath. Whichever method you choose, stick with it for the whole session, or there will be too much thinking about it and changing your mind.

So, be lightly aware of the breath. Only the breath.

When thoughts arise, like: 'I'll never be able to do this; I should have chosen the abdomen; what is the time now?'

Simply acknowledge the thought, with no blame, let it go and return to the breath.

Whatever the thought, acknowledge thinking, with no blame, allow it to be, then gently let the thought go and return to the breath.

If a sensation arises, a pain or an itch maybe, simply acknowledge sensation, let it go and return to the breath.

Just the breath.

If the sensation is still there and doesn't dissolve on its own, then let the pain or whatever it is become the object of the meditation. Focus on the pain, explore the pain without pushing it away. The pure sensation, with no storyline is so different, it is sensation, just sensation. *With* the storyline it becomes suffering, without it, just sensation.

Staying with the sensation.

Then return to the breath.

The more you have to return to the breath, the more practice you get; you are training and taming the mind.

If the sensation is too troublesome and you wish to move, *decide* to move and then move consciously.

Return to the breath.

More thoughts, multiple sensations, simply let them go into the great ocean of mind. They are just passing show.

Returning always to the breath.

Gently focused on the breath.

Observe thoughts arising and falling away, sensations arising and falling away. If the thought takes you somewhere else, when you realise you have gone, simply acknowledge the thought, with no blame at all, no judging, then let it go. Easy. And return to the breath.

Just the breath.

Keep returning to the breath.

Allow the breath to become a haven. Notice that the thoughts of the future hold anxiety and the thoughts of the past have guilt and despair attached, the present is just as it is. Be in the present, and the breath is all that is happening in the present.

Just the breath.

Sink into the haven of the breath. Notice that thoughts cause emotional turbulence, excitement, anxiety, sadness. The thoughts hype you up or bring you down. The breath has no story, the breath just is.

Sink into the breath, the neutrality of the breath. There are no emotions associated with the breath.

The breath becomes safe.

Let go of thoughts. You can't be bothered with your stuff at the moment. You don't need your story right now, you can pick it up later, it will wait for you. There is only the breath right now, the light spaciousness of the breath. The truth of the breath.

Whatever the thought, acknowledge thinking, let it go, return to the safety of the breath.

The breath becomes home.

Surrender into the breath.

The joy of just surrendering. The ease and the peace, nothing but the simple breath.

Notice that the breath may be becoming finer at this point. The breath may even be hard to find. As the breath decreases you may notice a beautiful sensation arising, you can use this wonderful bliss state as the object of your focus, your meditation. Almost no breath, just the bliss. You are filled with bliss. You are in the environment of bliss.

Just focus on the bliss. Surrender into the bliss. So easy to do, so delightful. The mind is at home, the mind doesn't want to be anywhere else.

Allow the mind to rest in this arising bliss, the moment. Enjoy the sensation, the buoyant delight of the now. Surrender utterly into your Self. So safe, so endless, so pure. Pure delight, pure bliss filling everywhere you are.

This is meditation, this is reality, no frills, this is easy.

TO COME OUT OF MEDITATION

Become aware of your surroundings.

Deepen your breathing slightly.

Move your fingers and your toes.

Smile with pleasure.

And in your own time, gently open your eyes

NOTES ON THE MEDITATION

The loving-kindness beginning of the meditation is a reminder that compassion brings contentment.

I was talking with a visiting Tibetan lama in York. And of course Tibetan monks devote their lives to cultivating wisdom and compassion.

He had mentioned that there were no other monks with whom he could live so he lived with some lay friends in Sheffield.

"So have I got this right," I said, "you are the *only* monk of your particular lineage in the UK?"

"Yes," he said.

I made an involuntary, concerned, "Oh" at the sadness of being the only one.

And he responded, "Oh," perfectly mimicking my concern.

And we giggled in delight, like two schoolgirls.

We both got the subtext.

He was taking the mickey. He was gently mocking my misplaced compassion because he was doing fine, practicing the cultivation of wisdom and compassion amongst us ordinary folk. Life was just grist for his mill.

And he was aware that my concern was showing the feelings that I thought I would have in his shoes, therefore illustrating where I was so limited – and wrong. And I was aware of that too and found it so funny that one little "Oh" and its echo said it all.

He was amazing, so wise and so simple, joyous and compassionate. That's what loving-kindness can do.

I added the arising of bliss at the end of the meditation practice because that is, in fact, the natural order of things. If you surrender sufficiently into the breath, into the now, the breath becomes finer, more shallow, as your metabolic rate goes down. This is, in part, why meditation is so good for you. It lowers high blood pressure, slows things down and allows calm and repair.

As the breath gets finer, there is less breath on which to focus. It's OK because as this happens, the first jhana, the first altered state of consciousness, arises, the state of bliss. You therefore focus on the bliss instead of the breath, which has almost disappeared. The bliss is so delightful that the mind naturally wants to reside in it. So meditation becomes a pleasure. It is now easy to meditate. There is nowhere else you would rather be at this moment than here, focusing on bliss.

These altered states are not a goal, or end in themselves, but they are lovely and do help you to stay on the meditation cushion as you had planned.

And don't worry that this is so seductive that you will want to drop out of society, become a meditation junky and never wash again. Look at me: lawyer, wife, acupuncturist, dog-walker... I am living proof that working, domestic, Yorkshire life still goes on despite (or is that because of) daily meditation. (And I'm very clean.)

Meditation is not just good for you, but for everyone else too. (Ask my husband! On a bad day he has been known to suggest, through gritted teeth, that I go upstairs to meditate – and presumably come down again when I'm nicer.)

You do get so that your *good* vibes can change the atmosphere in a room for the better, rather like a couple's unspoken anger and resentment can, but for the worse.

The TM (transcendental meditation) people do research on meditation and they gathered thousands of meditators together in, I think, Chicago and found that, for the duration of their retreat, the crime rate went down significantly. See, we all need you to do this.

Should this sound far too esoteric and downright impossible, something else extraordinary happened to me at that eventful first Ram Dass retreat. Let me explain.

10

Who needs a guru?

It was whilst I was at that first RD retreat that I encountered a guru and I have to say, I didn't like it. I was wrong (yet again) and feel we should explore the phenomenon of the guru.

First of all, is your own guru necessary?

Well no, but any help along the boulder-strewn path is a boost. They don't call it 'the road less travelled' for nothing. It can seem pretty lonely when you are asking questions about life (and beyond life) whilst your friends are worrying about the cost of liposuction, on the way to the pub.

At a party in my village I was trying to explain to someone what I'd got out of a recent retreat, the host of the party overheard me, saying: "You just weren't there when ordinary was handed out, were you Sal?" It's not true, of course, there are a lot of ordinary folk looking for answers.

There aren't a huge number of people who can help you with those answers though, so people who are pondering the ultimate questions tend to value the idea of a guru, someone looking out for them and perhaps pointing them in the right direction.

The trouble is you can't go and *find* a guru. You could visit an ashram found on the internet and it might be lovely, but it probably wouldn't be ultimately satisfying. The truth is that the guru finds you.

By the time I came across Ram Dass, his guru, Neem Karoli Baba, had been dead for about 14 years. His powers were unabated however, and the little matter of not having a body seemed to be no curb at all, as I was to find out.

It was my birthday and my treat had been to attend this wonderful retreat in the South of France with Ram Dass. The only fly in the ointment was that he had a huge picture of the guru up on the side of the podium where he sat to speak to us. I'd never heard of his guru and found myself really discomforted by the picture.

Ram Dass was charming and funny and wise. I was captivated. He had Jai Lakshman along to chant with us, Jai had the voice and demeanour of an angel and he brought such devotion to the chants that it was impossible not to 'get it'.

I was as happy as it is possible to be, except for that picture, and Ram Dass's constant references to his guru ("Don't listen to me, I talk to a fat, old (dead) Indian guy! Sheer neurosis!").

I had been complaining over lunch to a chum and he said I should enjoy Ram Dass and Jai, and relax into that, I didn't need to buy the whole package. I agreed, but said that I couldn't understand how anyone as intelligent as Ram Dass could be so involved with a Hindu miracle worker. My friend just said that it was his path, and it didn't need to be mine.

Too right, I thought.

So the retreat passed in a haze, in the middle of which we had a few days of silence where we were not allowed to speak to each other or even look at another person in the eyes. On my birthday a lady came and silently put some early blackberries she had picked from hedgerows into my hands, it was lovely.

The girls in my dorm had clubbed together and they presented me with a book of stories about the guru called *Miracle of Love*. It was all done up with dental floss and flowers, it looked so beautiful. I was very touched.

Pity about the book though.

Some months later, back at home, after seriously overworking, I became ill. Nobody was too sure what it was, but I was in a sorry state in bed and refusing to go into hospital. If I was going to die it was going to be in my own home.

The illness reached a crisis point and I was lying in bed at night in a great deal of pain almost drowning in the secretions in my chest, too weak to cough. I was confused and very agitated. My husband was sleeping next door so I would not be disturbed.

Suddenly there was a change in the room, my agitated mind became completely calm and very clear. I 'saw' a figure wrapped in a white blanket sitting on the end of the bed to the left with just a foot sticking out, the foot had a red toenail on the big toe. There was another figure to the right, but I wasn't focused on that, I was mesmerised by the blanketed figure. Whilst the guru was always wrapped in a blanket, it was usually plaid, and this was white, but I knew instantly it was him.

In my mind I said, 'I'm very surprised to see you, because I don't believe in you.' He continued to sit there with his back to me, immobile. Probably looking bored. But the atmosphere in the room was amazing. It was like the beginnings of a giggle, sheer delight. It was as if you were poised on the point of laughter and were able to remain in that state all night long. It was wonderful.

The next morning my husband, who was worried to death about me, came in and said, "You look different." I just managed to whisper that it was wonderful, and that was that.

I knew enough from Vipassana training to know that you can't hang onto things. If the things have changed you, then that is who you are, and there is nothing to hold onto. So I didn't grab onto the feeling to make it stay, I sort of bathed in it whilst it was there. Slowly, over three days, it subsided.

But *I had* changed, for sure.

I phoned the chum from the retreat and told him. He laughed and laughed, "You've been collected," he said. I was astonished, thinking that it had just been a one off. But I was interested enough to read one story a day from *Miracle of Love* over the next three months of my recovery. And sure enough the quality of the guru shown in the pages was just the quality I had experienced in the room. He had the feeling of delight, naughtiness and fun alongside a fierce spiritual devotion to Ram.

Or had I imagined it all?

It is still a surprise to me that, when I'm in need, he's there.

For instance, I had to have an MRI scan on my knee. I was worrying because the magnetic radiation of the scan was allegedly 30,000 times that of the earth's magnetic field. I was lying in the tube anxious that my pineal gland, in my head, would be affected. My tortuous logic was that birds navigate by their pineal gland as a way of detecting the magnetic field of the earth, so the pineal must be incredibly sensitive to magnetism. I also knew that the pineal was reputed to be involved in healing. As I worked as a healer, I needed my pineal gland, and would it be damaged?

I had got myself into a tangled knot of fear before the procedure and now the metal of the huge scanner was about two inches from my face and body with some God-awful noise going on. Suddenly there was this huge, fat Indian man sitting on my thighs, between my pineal and the knee, where all the action was.

I was so shocked.

There's no room for you in here.

I felt instantly claustrophobic, having managed not to be up to then. Then I got it, and realised that he didn't need any room, and that this was amazing and he wasn't really real, except that he was, and he was here. It was great.

I also was somewhat astonished that he should bother to collect me, when I hadn't exactly been drawn to him in the first place. But then I remembered the last day of that retreat.

We had been chanting the names of God, for hours. The chant, led by Jai Lakshman, would be Rama, Rama, Rama, so simple and so beautiful, then the deity would be changed, Allah, Allah, Allah, or Jesu, Jesu, Jesu etc. I had found myself opening and opening. It was as if I thought, 'Oh what the hell. I'll just surrender to all of it.'

I had enjoyed the teachings, the meditation and the Tai Chi, so why not go for it and allow myself to surrender into Ram?

And I did. I got it. I was lost in love and surrender, safety and absolute trust. I stood up at one point, and had my arms above my head. Tears were streaming down my face as I surrendered so utterly into all these aspects of God, and Ram in particular.

Here I should add that Neem Karoli Baba is intimately connected to Ram in the story of the *Ramayana*. Surrender into Ram was his life's occupation.

So I guess that was it. If you are open, and surrendered, the guru has no choice but to come to you, even if you are a misery-guts, full of doubts and judgements.

A friend later sent me a picture of that time, with the waving arms, the tears, the upturned face and the beatific smile. It's a photo reserved for the chosen few, I can tell you. It could put you off your tea.

But inside, oh my, so beautiful.

SO HOW DID RAM DASS ACQUIRE THE GURU?

Ram Dass was brought to his guru in a typically bizarre way. He was always a bright boy and was holding simultaneous professorships at Harvard and Yale.

He had been doing research into the effects of magic mushrooms as, at the time, taking them was legal. He'd had the experience of his consciousness being altered and just wanted more.

Because he had carried on his 'research' after the drugs were made illegal, he had eventually been sacked from both of his professorships.

Yet despite his keen interest in mushrooms, he noticed that no matter how high he got, he always had to come down. This bugged him. He was also aware that there were people in India who 'knew', and who didn't need mushrooms.

Those people could alter their consciousness and go to the places that he could go to, but without the aid of drugs. And they could control it – go there, stay there and come back at will.

So he went to India and did some wandering. He had an encounter with a young man, Bagvan Das who needed a lift to visit his guru. Ram Dass had a borrowed car and Bagvan Das drove them there. It turned out that the guru was up on a hillside and a delighted Bagvan Das was prostrating himself in ecstasy before him. Ram Dass was angry, paranoid and preoccupied, worrying that someone would steal the car.

The guru looked totally bored (he never behaved himself) and suggested to Ram Dass through an interpreter that he was a rich American, and should give him the car. Basically, he was pushing Ram Dass's buttons, and pissing him off.

Then he said something very surprising. He said, "You were out under the stars last night." Ram Dass *had* been, but he was unimpressed, an easy guess he thought.

Then the guru said, "You were thinking about your mother." Now this did rattle Ram Dass. He had got up to go for a pee in the night and had lingered in the garden on his way back to his room, looking up at the stars, and he had indeed been thinking about his mother, and her death.

The guru whispered, "She got very fat before she died," and then he said, in English, the word '*Spleen*'. And Ram Dass flipped. His mother had developed ascites, a very swollen abdomen, before she died of cancer of the spleen, and this had been very distressing for him. But how did this rural Indian know?

Ram Dass's mind did somersaults trying to rationalise this turn of events. But he hardly knew Bagvan Das, and he certainly hadn't discussed his mother with him. He knew there were CIA files on him. Had this Indian man got access to information? It was very unlikely, if not impossible. There was no internet back then, the guru hadn't known he was coming and couldn't have known who he was.

The guru was close to him looking into his eyes with a gaze that was so devastatingly loving that

Ram Dass just cried. He cried and cried – for days. He was taken away and looked after. There were other devotees looking on with sympathy, having been through similar ordeals of fire themselves.

And so he was – 'collected'.

The name of his guru is of course Neem Karoli Baba and Ram Dass has written the book of stories about him called *Miracle of Love*.

Suffice it to say that the guru was a thoroughly rascally fellow of unknown antiquity who got his name as a young man when he was a wandering sadhu, or holy man. He was put off a train for not having a ticket. The train had been stopped at a village called Neem Karori and the sadhu was put off. There was no station there and he just sat quietly on the dirt.

The train driver was unable to get the train going. After a considerable time, one of the passengers said to the ticket inspector that perhaps it had been a mistake to throw a holy man off the train. Eventually they went to him and begged him to get back on the train, and to make the train go. The young sadhu shrugged and said, "What do I know about running trains?" But he did agree to get back on the train, after securing a promise that the railroad company would build a station for the people of Neem Karori. As soon as he was back on board, the train got underway.

He was thoroughly unreliable and an astonishing miracle worker with terrific powers, which he was adept at concealing. He would always deny that he had worked the miracle and would say of whoever was reporting the incident, "Don't believe him, he's a liar!"

I think it is safe to say that we would consider him bonkers should we bump into him now.

11

The *Ramayana* for dummies

I think at this point it would be good to give you a very potted version of the *Ramayana*, a holy Hindu text, so that you can get a feel for the sort of beings these great saints, or gurus are. Also it serves as a reminder of holy stories commonly found in other traditions.

It is said that my guru, Neem Karoli Baba was linked with, or an incarnation of, Hanuman, the monkey god from the *Ramayana*, and so Ram Das loves this story and told it to us at my first retreat with him.

Now I found all this 'incarnation of Hanuman' stuff a bit hard to take, but when enough things happen in my life that point to a truth, eventually I will pay attention. And the guru seems to be a regular and surprising presence in my life, and not a little miraculous, unruly and monkey-ish. So who knows?

For instance, we were in India on holiday and found ourselves staying in a palace, on our way to somewhere else. And what a palace.

The Maharaja's Eton-educated son, who ran the family palace as an hotel, took a shine to me when he noticed that I'd quietly healed a French tourist after he had leant on a hornet. His palm had been stung. Poor bloke.

There was great big hole in his palm and God knows what pain he was suffering. Anyway, the Frenchman's pain went and the Maharaja's son nodded as if this was run of the mill.

"She's a healer," he shrugged.

Later, we got talking and when questioned, I said who my guru was, it's like a shorthand, and saved a lot of explanations. He wondered if we would like to go to a temple that was a Hanuman temple that afternoon, he was taking a group of French tourists, and we had a driver who could take us separately.

The temple was a dank cave with a huge Shiva lignum (whopping phallus) inside. Didn't do anything for me, I have to say. Still, outside at the back was a beautiful lake with *orange* peacocks strutting about. I was drawn to a huge sloping rock that gently shelved to meet the water.

Sitting on the warm rock, I was feeling peaceful, and a bit spacey, when the Maharaja's son found us. He said he thought I would be in this spot because this was where the God of the Wind had gone up the skirt of Hanuman's mother and impregnated her, and Hanuman was born instantly, ready formed. (It's a God thing, obviously.)

There had been plenty of other places to hang out, so I found it interesting that I chose this one, or rather, was drawn to it.

WHY TELL THE STORY OF THE *RAMAYANA*?

It's just really auspicious, as well as a cracking story.

The *Ramayana* is all about Hanuman, and his relationship to Ram.

Apparently every time it is told it is a great boon, and they say that the monkey god, Hanuman, is always present in the telling. So just keep your eyes open.

THE STORY

The story starts with a demon king called Ravana behaving very badly on earth and the Gods up in Heaven getting mighty peed off with him. He is wreaking havoc, has a whopping great stronghold on the island of Sri Lanka, and a whole demon army with which to create mayhem.

In the Hindu pantheon, the main trio of God is: Bramha, the creator; Vishnu the preserver; and Shiva the destroyer. The Gods looked down at what was going on, and Vishnu decided to come to Earth as Ram to try and sort out Ravana.

Ram is a prince with a wonderful father, the king, and great brothers. Ram is the perfect son and the perfect prince, as you can imagine, him being God and all. He marries Sita who is the perfect wife and it's all looking lovely.

Ram is the eldest son and is set to inherit the kingdom on the retirement of the king, however the night before the big ceremony one of the king's other wives calls in a boon from him.

He owed her.

Apparently she had saved the king's life after an injury on the battlefield and now it was payback time. She managed to convince him that Ram was up to no good, that her own son should be put on the throne and Ram should be exiled in the woods.

The king had to agree to her request and instead of the morning dawning on his coronation as king, Ram was off into exile with his wife Sita. Being the perfect son of course he didn't demure and just said, "Of course, father, whatever you wish."

Well, it's a holy story.

Another brother Lakshmi is so concerned for his brother that he goes into exile with Ram and Sita.

So there they are, the three of them hanging out in the forest, happy and contented. But then (there is always a but) Ravana sees them and thinks that Sita is really hot. Fellow demons warn him off, you don't mess with God's wife they say, but he is determined.

Ravana is cunning and disguises himself as a wounded deer. He runs past the clearing where they are in their hut. Sita insists that Ram go after the deer to help, which he does, but before he goes he draws a circle around the hut and tells Sita that she is protected, provided she stays inside the circle.

Of course things don't go too well, and Lakshmi has to go into the forest and find Ram. He's not worried about leaving Sita because she is in the circle.

But then... the resourceful Ravana disguises himself as an old man who staggers past the hut (you almost get to like him don't you?). Sita is full of compassion and when she gives him the water he asks for, she steps out of the circle, is grabbed by the now powerful Demon King and whisked away on his flying chariot to his stronghold in Sri Lanka.

Poor old Sita throws jewels and bracelets down to act as a trail, but to no avail. Ram and Lakshmi come back to find her gone, with a deficit in the clue-department.

The search is on.

Now back to the heavenly realms. Whilst Vishnu is incarnated as Ram, Shiva looks down and sees the might of Ravana growing and decides to help Ram. He incarnates as ... ta da... Hanuman the monkey god, son of the Wind. Up the skirt on the rock and wham bam, there he is.

Now the thing about Hanuman is that he is very powerful (Shiva no less) but he doesn't know it, because he's a monkey. All he knows is that he is completely and utterly devoted to Ram.

Ram is searching everywhere for Sita and everyone, even the animals, are helping him.

Hanuman has the feeling that he knows where she is but he looks across at Lanka and doesn't know how to get there. The other animals tell him that he is so powerful, the son of the Wind and all, that he can jump the space across the water easily.

He is surprised by this.

He says that if he can, how will Sita know that he is a messenger from Ram? That's easy, Ram gives him his ring. Hanuman is to show it to Sita and she will know that she is not abandoned by Ram and that this is indeed a messenger from her husband.

On Lanka the demon hordes are holed up, and the fortress of Ravana is huge and impressive. Ravana is a great big, gorgeous demon. He's been strutting his stuff and has tried everything to woo Sita but she is not having any of it. Why have hamburger when you've known steak, I guess (except that they would all be vegetarian, but you get my drift, and it's not the same with a cabbage and aubergine analogue).

At the end of his patience, Ravana has given her a few more days and then if she is not willing to be his consort, he'll bump her off.

Sita is in distress, wandering forlornly in the Oshoka groves.

Meanwhile Hanuman is persuaded that he can leap to Lanka, and in the Charles Buck version of the *Ramayana* there's wonderful description of his mighty leap creating such a wind that the seas parted leaving fish exposed 'like people surprised at home'.

And there he is in Sri Lanka. Losing no time, he turns himself into his tiny form so as not to frighten Sita as he approaches her. He shows her Ram's ring and convinces her that he is from Ram and that he has an army of monkeys to help her.

Her objection at this point is that even if he got them there, if they were all as small as him, the size of a mosquito, what could they do against the mighty Ravana?

Hanuman puffs himself up instantly to become hugely tall and powerful, a wonderful specimen of monkey. She's impressed.

Of course he is then caught by Ravana's guards and brought before Ravana.

As an emissary of Ram, Hanuman suggests that Ravana might want to let Sita go – like now. Ravana isn't impressed and wants to kill Hanuman. (Hell of a boy that Ravana.) Well, the rules are that you can't kill an emissary. But you can maybe hurt him a bit.

Ravana realises that monkeys are very fond of their tails so he has Hanuman's tail wrapped in cloth and then set on fire. Thing is that as they are wrapping, Hanuman's tail grows and grows so there is a lot of cloth and therefore a lot of fire when they were done.

Hanuman runs off, setting fire to the whole of Lanka, becoming small to get out of the burning bandages, and then hopping it back to India.

Once it is known that Sita is there all of the animals drop stones and rocks and boulders into the sea making a great causeway across to Lanka. It is said that Ram was so pleased with the work of the chipmunk that he stroked it and it has had a stripe down its back ever since.

Ram and his army swarm across to take Lanka and reclaim the lovely Sita.

There is a great battle to be fought the next day and things aren't looking too good for Ravana.

That night on the battlements *Death* comes to Ravana, telling him that though he's had a good time, the game is now up and he can't cheat Death. Ravana laughs at him. Death is most put out and asks why he is laughing, because Death will most certainly have him tomorrow in the battle.

It turns out that Ravana has been granted a boon from the Gods that he can't be killed. Ravana has stipulated all of the realms from which he is protected, but has omitted the human realm, thinking humans not worthy of consideration. This was why Vishnu incarnated as a human.

So Death has a point, Ram is in human form and Ravana is on borrowed time.

Then Ravana comes out with a corker. It seems that as a demon he can't be taken up to heaven by the Gods. The only way that can happen, is for him to be killed by God.

So, not as daft as he looks. He isn't bad, he just wants eternal life and to escape the wheel of life and death. He has behaved appallingly for a purpose, to get God, Ram, to kill him.

Makes you think, dunnit? Who are we to judge anything, we can't know anyone's karmic story.

Anyway, sure enough Ram is victorious and goes back home in triumph. His wonderful brother vacates the throne, only ever having viewed himself as a caretaker, apparently.

Ram cannot thank the monkey Hanuman enough and gives him a ring. The monkey is disdainful. He bites it and destroys it saying it is useless as the name of Ram is nowhere inside it.

It is then pointed out that Hanuman himself must fall into the same category, not having the name of Ram running through his body. At which point Hanuman tears open his own chest to reveal the name of Ram, Ram, Ram, Ram on every bone and sinew.

Now that's devotion to God.

RAM, RAM, RAM

This explains why Neem Karoli Baba, or Maharaji, with his close links to Hanuman the monkey, was always so steeped in Ram. He would just chant the name of Ram constantly.

A local Indian official came to the ashram one time, and fainted. He had seen the guru as a huge monkey. Certainly there are many pictures of Maharaji sitting with his arms bending the wrong way with something definitely of the monkey about him.

It would also explain the naughtiness and monkey-like mischievousness of the guru. He would never admit to his miracles, always creating a smokescreen of confusion, and often abuse. He would generally shout and swear at people to leave the ashram for no apparent reason and hurl a lot of fruit about. A very unruly monkey.

He wasn't into meditation much either, his own practice was total surrender and service to Ram. When asked by devotees how to become enlightened, he would say: "Serve the people"; when asked: "No seriously now, how can I become enlightened?" the reply would be, "feed the people". Mind you he did also suggest you should bring your mind to one point and wait for grace, there'd be a bit of meditation needed there then.

Despite his unruly behaviour, he had limitless compassion and he did have the most terrific powers, and still does. He is revered as a great saint in India and is dearly beloved by an immense number of devotees.

Jai Lakshman, the man who did the wonderful chanting, became a devotee through knowing Ram Dass, way after the Guru had left the body.

One day at an ashram in the States, Jai flipped. He thought: 'What am I doing here with all these people? I'm an ordinary boy from Brooklyn'. And he got in his car and just drove away.

He drove for hours and eventually found himself at some hotel on the coast at two in the morning. He was in the lobby chatting to the guy behind the counter because he had to wait for someone to check out before he could have a room.

After some time the concierge said that he had something for Jai, he came round the desk and gave him an envelope which Jai opened to find a picture of Maharaji. The concierge told him that a fat old Indian man had left it for him that afternoon.

A bit of me was inclined to put this story down to wishful thinking, sceptical as ever. But then:

There I was at a Ram Dass retreat and I very much wanted a big picture of the guru for myself (this was pre-internet and the instant downloading of pictures). I asked the two ladies who helped with Ram Dass's administration, but they said they only had some little ones to give out at the end of the retreat. I was disappointed because for some reason I wanted a large picture of him.

One afternoon a few of us were lying on the floor listening to stories that Jai was telling about the guru. Jai was collating the stories to go into another book. He was amused that we were so laid back (knackered was nearer the mark). As we were leaving the room I stopped Jai to ask him about some detail of a story that had caught my attention so that I could write it down. Outside in the corridor he opened his file to shuffle through his papers and find the story. There was a big, gorgeous, picture of Maharaji tucked into the inside cover of the file. Jai got it out and gave it to me absent-mindedly.

I thanked him profusely and said I had wanted a picture. He said, "Oh right, I wondered why I was giving it to you, it's the only one I have!"

12

Am I doing it right?
Synchronicity and pointers
along the way

There's really only one thing to do when it comes to meditation, and that is to surrender. You surrender who you think you are – your great fat, sticky, gorgeous, horrible storyline into this moment. The object of your surrender could be the breath, a guru, a dot, endless space, or your Rupert Bear pyjama case, whatever it is, focus on it, settle in, come into the moment and let the mind calm down.

Surrender encompasses, and is included in, all sorts of paths that have been trodden before us, and they seem to work – so we can choose a path and method to which we are drawn, and surrender, trying it on for size. Then, whatever your method, rather miraculously, as you calm down you notice things.

You get intuitive feelings as you go about your business, and you find that if you follow them, it all works out surprisingly well. You get synchronous happenings, just when you most need them.

You begin to feel the benign power of love around you as you stay open to it, surrendered, grateful and still.

Maybe it's not all a ghastly mistake, maybe you're actually where you are supposed to be.

As you get more into your intuition and synchronous, even quite miraculous, things pop up, you get the insight that it may even be safe to relax.

Wow. What would that do for your stress levels and BP?

A HOME-GROWN EXAMPLE OF HOW IT WORKS

One beautiful morning I was down by the river close to my home and I was looking out over the fields on the other side of the river. I saw a dead tree in the distance on whose skeletal branches were several herons, all perching with their necks stretched up to impossible heights. They looked wonderful in their roost.

I was very quiet, looking at them. I whispered, maybe not even out loud, 'There's no difference between you and me. We are all one. You can be here with me and I can see you clearly.'

I imagined a heron flying over to me and landing in front of me, I imagined seeing it up close and in detail. There really was, in that moment, no distance between us and no difference between us, it was as if all was one.

Nothing happened.

I felt a bit silly, but disappointed, it had been so vivid.

After lunch I was at the river again, about 100 yards downstream from my morning daydream, and staring at the sparkling water, again utterly in the moment. It was stunning.

Suddenly I heard a whoosh, whoosh and there was a heron flying up the river like a Lancaster bomber.

It was enormous and it flew so close that I could see its long neck sort of folded and tucked in and its legs and feet tucked up. It looked huge and chunky in flight. As I watched, it unfolded itself and landed, tall and willowy now, on exactly the spot where I had been standing three hours earlier.

It made me laugh as I acknowledged that the arrival of the bird in the morning would have spooked me. This was a good old synchronicity, with a respectable time delay, but it still felt miraculous and rather humbling. I felt such love and gratitude for that bird, and a bit apologetic for putting it to the trouble.

Then I thought, no, it's all an inevitability. Life *had* to bring me the heron, it was the law somehow, just what happens when you are in tune with the Universe.

I felt in awe, and hoped it found some fish.

WHERE YOU ARE CAN BE MAGIC

It's all a state of mind really.

Wonderful, surreal things happen anywhere and any time. It really is a measure of your surrender into the moment.

I was walking with my dog, some years ago through the fields near to my house, next to a nicely maturing beech copse surrounded by a tall fence with rabbit-proof netting around it. Nowhere exotic, just home.

It was an early evening in summer, I was on my own for a week with no suppers to cook and I was enjoying the luxury of time.

My progress was slow, my dog being old and patient with me as I wandered. I was feeling expansive and loving, blessed to be in a beautiful place, nurtured and cocooned by nature.

Suddenly in front of me was this wonderful stag. Quite big, surprisingly, and with an impressive set of antlers.

We just stood staring at each other about ten feet apart. I was spellbound and felt this enormous loving communication with this wild and magnificent creature.

The dog lay down.

We must have communed together for minutes, the stag and I, maybe only two or three, but it seemed like forever. It all felt normal and natural, just two beings, together.

Then I went and ruined the surrender into that moment.

Suddenly I had thoughts about other people and the vulnerability of the stag. Instead of allowing the magical moment to unfold as it would I was thinking things like: 'You shouldn't be here; this isn't safe for you; people aren't safe.' I was trying to control life instead of being in the flow of it.

Straight away the stag lowered his head a little and just jumped sideways right up and over the fence and into the copse, from a standing start! It trotted into the thick of the copse and out of sight. I felt blessed and a little bereft. I wanted him to stay.

Me and my big thought! Damn.

HOW DID THAT CHANT GO?

I had been intending to choose a meditation at this point on the Tibetan Lama, Padmasambhava with a chant to him to illustrate the devotion and surrender to a guru by chanting and how magical that can be wherever you are. I couldn't remember the Indian version of the chant, as I now use the Tibetan version. But I knew it would come to me so didn't think about it any more.

A little later, on a different point, I was looking in the bookshelf for a particular book on Guru meditation in the Theravadan Buddhist tradition as opposed to the Tibetan tradition and couldn't find it. However, I put my hand on a book by a Tibetan lama, Sogyal Rinpoche, *The Tibetan Book of Living and Dying* and it fell open at a picture of Padmasambhava, opposite which was an explanation of guru meditation – including the two versions of the chant. Just what I had been looking for earlier.

I must have been open and surrendered to the moment.

So there was synchronicity.

What I'm suggesting is that a few experiences of synchronicity can encourage you to see that it is all unfolding as it should. You might as well take your foot off the accelerator and enjoy the ride. (When I've mastered the art I'll let you know.)

OPENING TO AN IMAGE

I had in fact been reading that same book, *The Tibetan Book of Living and Dying,* whilst travelling round India with my husband on holiday years ago. We were above Dharamshala where the Tibetan government in exile is based. We were in a small village nestled below the snow-capped Himalayas and whilst there was a big temple, there were dirt streets and a series of tiny shacks by the road selling various goods.

Having reached the page in the book with the chant I've just mentioned, I'd never come across the two versions of the chant before, I wondered about the Tibetan pronunciation, tune and rhythm. Meandering into a kiosk, there, staring at me was the same book in the form of a tape set (it was a very long time ago). So hey presto, I could listen as well as read on my travels *and* hear the chant in both versions. Thank you.

In the temple I found a gold *statue* of Padmasambhava. I sat for a long time cross-legged on the floor in front of the statue. It was the size of a small man, the image of the guru made in the eighth century. It was a seated figure with painted features. It had eyebrows that curled upwards in a stylised way, staring eyes and a split moustache, shown by curly lines either side of his cheeks giving him the look of an ancient Hercule Poirot.

I knew that Padmasambhava had introduced Buddhism into Tibet where others had failed, and was called the second Buddha as a consequence. I knew that he was more powerful than the indigenous shamans of the Bon religion in Tibet and was known affectionately as Guru Rinpoche, or Precious Master by the Tibetans.

So he must be special, right?

Tibetan women with dusters on their hands and feet were prostrating themselves full length on the floor, then standing up so their feet were where their hands had been, then bending down and doing it all over again. They made slow progress round the temple but the end of the trip was the space in front of the statue of Padmasambhava.

Their devotion was amazing. I knew the Tibetans had carried this statue all the way across the perilous Himalayas, an incredible journey for the people, never mind the people plus a heavy statue.

Nevertheless, I was strangely unimpressed by this funny looking painted statue and wondered why they had bothered (sorry to admit this). I mean I even knew that this statue had been imbued with power by Guru Rinpoche himself: when it was being made he came by and said, "Looks like me." Then he is said to have touched it, saying, "*Is* me."

So I sat for ages, but it was pearls before swine as far as I was concerned. I bought a postcard of the image from a street vendor on my way out, but that was effectively that.

Later I was wandering around, down dirt roads past small dwellings and I started to chant gently to Padmasambhava, remembering the comical look of the statue from the morning.

The chant is: Om Ah Hum Vajra Guru Padma Siddhi Hum. Except that the Tibetans chant: Om Ah Hung *Benza* Guru *Pema* Siddhi Hung. So I chose the Tibetan pronunciation, when in Rome…

I was walking slowly and chanting under my breath to the Guru with no expectations, but a great deal of humility as I had terrific respect for the Tibetans, when suddenly I found myself surrounded by a bubble, like a vacuum, filled with immense *presence*. I was shocked. Power filled me, and the air around me. It was like a *blast*, not a genteel experience, this was bad-boy, hardcore, scary power.

In fact, this was so not gentle, it was like being caught in an electric grip. It was thrilling and awe-inspiring. I was transfixed.

Dazed and thunderstruck, I now understood why the women prostrated, I'd have prostrated all the way from Tibet to get that feeling.

So it's good to remember that not only images, but sounds, have an effect on us. The *words* of ancient chants themselves have immense power.

Careless chants change lives!

THE POWER OF SOUNDS

It was another egg-on-my-face moment, and came as a result of a trip to the temple of the Emerald Buddha in Thailand, again on holiday with my long-suffering husband. I was mesmerised but contemptuous (that judging again), of the actual statue of the Buddha. It was solid emerald and set up high, but actually quite small when seen from below, as you would expect for something made from a single emerald. After the huge golden Thai Buddhas seen in other temples it looked insignificant.

I sat on the floor as parties of schoolchildren filed in and out and monks and nuns came and went. It was a busy place. Nothing happened to me and back in the sunshine I felt fine and bought a book of chants to the Emerald Buddha from a street vendor. (I do this you notice, it's called Spiritual Materialism.) It was a thin book containing one very long chant written in Pali. I had chanted a bit in Pali in the monastery in Chang Mai where my daughter had been a nun, so was a little bit familiar with it.

Weeks later, back home in England, I decided to do the chant. It was a quiet morning so I sat down and began.

I had no idea what I was chanting, but felt excited and privileged to be able to do it. It was a slow rather difficult process to get my English tongue around the words but I liked it and was open to the lilting sound of the Pali.

It went on and on. I was getting a bit fed up, only halfway through the booklet, and I needed a pee. So I got up to go to the bathroom thinking maybe I'd go downstairs for a cup of tea.

Then it hit me.

It was like walking into a solid wall, which wrapped round me almost hugging me, taking my breath away.

It made me think of a TV advert years ago for a building society with a castellated tower and a big hand coming over the top and knocking on the wall of the tower with a voice saying, 'Get the strength of the .... Building Society around you'. I later saw it outside a church rewritten as: 'Get the strength of Jesus around you'. And that's exactly what it was, I had the strength of the Emerald Buddha around me.

It was so astonishing that I rather shamefacedly agreed with myself to return after the comfort break to finish the chant, even though it now felt sacrilegious to be going to the loo at all.

THE POWER OF PLACES

Isn't it funny how places can become imbued with vibes from constant loving prayer or the holiness of relics housed there. I meditate everyday in the same place at home, in front of three pictures: my guru, Padmasambhava and Jesus. I get enormous comfort, just sitting down on my cushion. What terrific people to hang out with, and the repetition of meditation and love has built up a noticeable loving vibe too.

Also, our tiny village church is one of the nicest places to meditate, or just sit. It feels as if it has the presence of Jesus in it, but also the presence of all the love and prayer that has been practiced within that thousand year old space.

I can remember being in Assisi in Italy when the picture-perfect town, so carefully restored by the Vatican, was making me feel as if I were on a film set. It seemed not quite real, though gorgeous.

The church where the body of St Francis was interred was full of people, and again, lovely. I was grumbling to myself about him being a poor man and so simple – would he have wanted all this? (There I go again.)

Down in the crypt I sat on one of the chairs set out in serried ranks and tried just to *be* with the wonderful St Francis of Assisi. And suddenly – there was a most eloquent quality of simple peace, love and ineffable beauty which took me over. I was engulfed and entranced and just couldn't move. I would still be there now, had I been left.

Don't think though that you have to go to exotic places or adopt strange beliefs to have deep spiritual experience. Just surrender, where you are and to what is.

And my guru used to say that if you are of the west, Christ is your guru. Another time he said to meditate like Christ and when asked, how did Christ meditate, tears rolled down his face: "With all the love in the world," he said.

Of course sometimes we are a harder and more cynical nut to crack and our deepest selves seem to need to use desperate measures to get through to us. But it's only that we don't pay attention, we don't listen. The pointers are there.

You can do it the easy way and listen to your intuition, or the hard way following your head, and that way usually hurts.

Cynicism doesn't feel nearly as good as open-heartedness in any event.

LET'S TRY GURU MEDITATION

Just because we have been thinking of gurus and beings of power, wisdom, and love, wouldn't it be nice to get closer in and try a different form of surrender. This meditation may do the job.

To do the meditation just sit quietly in the meditation position, cross-legged on floor cushions or sitting in a chair with your back straight and a little way from the back of the chair. Lower your chin and lift your head creating space at the base of the head. Hands should be loosely in your lap. Take a few deep breaths and with each out-breath relax your shoulders.

With your eyes closed, imagine the figure of the deity or holy person, Jesus, Buddha, Padmasambhava, or whomever you choose, in front of you, sitting cross-legged on a lotus flower or cushion. In your mind, raise the image to the height of your eyes so that you are looking up behind your closed eyes to the head or heart of the deity.

Consider the qualities of the guru. Consider the love, compassion, and availability of the holy subject.

Contemplate the figure in detail. Smile and be open to accepting any experience that might happen.

Consider the specific attributes of the guru, his simplicity maybe, his love, his humour, or in the case of Padmasambhava his power and mighty calm. Think of all you know about the guru and consider each quality, allowing your heart to open to him.

Feel gratitude in your heart for this opportunity to have communion with so amazing a being. Be grateful even to be on the path of devotion.

Be thankful that this practice is even on your radar. It is given to so few to be open and humble enough to allow themselves to unlock their cynical hearts.

As you allow yourself to be in a state of gratitude, feel yourself opening more and more. Let the attributes of the guru be absorbed into your heart. Feel your heart swell and notice the experience.

Know that you are able to draw the guru into your heart or be drawn into the guru. Experience that union, every part of you filling with the power of the guru, allow yourself to be changed, taken over. Absorb all the wonderful qualities of this being whom you so revere.

Then just sit. Remain open, light. Have your attention lightly on the guru, feel playful, impressed, delighted. Just hang out.

You've got a great companion!

KEEP IT REAL

Before this sounds as if my life was one big woo-woo fest, it wasn't, it isn't. These are edited highlights, and I can and do lose the plot on a regular basis.

Recently I had been doing some healing on someone and, as I related it later to my husband, was feeling the next best thing to Jesus.

I was running late (again) for an appointment.

It took only five minutes and a trip though the wildly congested traffic and roadworks in the next village in my car, to have me gripping the steering wheel and shouting, out loud, at someone who was holding up the traffic by letting everyone, the whole world, in from each driveway and side road: "Stop being a knight of the f------ road, some of us are in hurry!"

My husband found this enormously funny.

Well, I never said I was prefect!

13

They're states Jim,
but not as we know them

Up to this point, my supercharged oneness was showing as moments that were random, but encouraging. Then something happened that brought it all to a new level and made it a practicable, codified and straightforward experience with a trajectory.

If it's codified and written down, it has to be Buddhist, right?

I was practicing Vipassana at home after being taught by Ram Dass on that first retreat in the South of France. I also went to a Thai Buddhist monastery here in England to learn more. I thought I'd got the hang of the practice, it put all my repetitive thoughts out of my mind for a while and gave me a degree of peace on a good day and intense frustration on a bad one.

Just when I was thinking that this intense focus on the breath might be getting easier, the most extraordinary thing happened.

I had taken my children to a playgroup in the morning. It had been particularly fraught, as only an echoing village hall with twenty under-fours plus loud toys, squash, crisps and a lot of shrieking can be. I came back feeling suitably strung out. So I took the emergency measure of parking the children in front of children's TV for ten minutes, taking myself off to my study at the other end of the hall to meditate and regain a bit of peace, with the door open as a precautionary measure.

I plonked myself down on my meditation cushion and desperately plunged into the breath. It was not so much total surrender as 'save me'.

The next thing I knew, I was super-conscious, super-aware, sparkling, like waking up to a crystal fountain in crisp air on a bright day.

I was suddenly engulfed in bliss and rapture. It was so real you could touch it.

I knew about letting things go in Vipassana, so I acknowledged bliss and mentally snapped my fingers to dismiss it. Instantly I went back to the breath, or tried to.

In fact as soon as I dismissed the bliss state I felt a huge surge of heart energy, a massive feeling of opening and softening in my chest, it was breath-taking. A mental click of the fingers and back to the breath – it was all I knew, all I had been taught.

Then a calm crossed my abdomen, which was soothed and felt sublime. Like putting a burden down, pure rightness and peace. Back to the breath.

Then my whole lower abdomen resonated with rightness, OK-ness, perfection. It was huge, as if my abdomen was expanding into a state of perfection and safety. Everything felt supercharged but so right, so expansive, like three glasses of red – with knobs on.

Back to the breath, those imaginary fingers were clicking away so fast, changing the states of consciousness. Each state was immense and all encompassing, almost bewildering. But mostly it was like being plugged into the mains.

I was then immediately plunged into the weirdest thing. I was in my head and the expansion was continuing only this time it was as if the sides of my head hinged downwards and my consciousness streamed out, forever. I thought the expansion would stop at the edges of the world but it didn't, it just went on.

Click of the mental fingers, back to the breath.

The infinite expanse again, only this time it was alive. It was conscious and infinite.

The breath.

Then – nothing. I mean really nothing. There was nothing and nowhere to stand, endless falling, with no landmarks, just empty. Infinite and empty. I recognised this place from childhood. Horror.

I couldn't go there, I felt that if I did I would lose who I was, my personality, and I would be permanently damaged. I wouldn't be able to function, I would have to be led around – I had two young children, I couldn't do this.

I opened my eyes, I was so frightened, I *couldn't* go back there.

So for months I was gripped by this paralyzing fear. I daren't shut my eyes in case it was there.

I was told it was the leap of a thousand Buddhas, but nobody I spoke to had experienced it. I couldn't meditate. At my next retreat with Ram Dass he told me to go to the edge of the nothingness and sit there, but I couldn't even sit on my cushion, never mind go to an edge.

Back at home a yoga teacher friend was on the phone discussing something purely social when I mentioned that I had just come back from a Ram Dass retreat.

She said, "I didn't know you meditated, you'll be interested in Ayya Khema, she's a Buddhist nun who is coming to give a talk to our yoga teacher's group in two weeks' time."

I *was* interested. I just knew I had to go and *I knew she knew*. It was in two weeks' time and only a few miles away from my home, how extraordinary.

So I turned up at a Friends Meeting House in a leafy suburb of York and sat on the floor with a variety of super-fit yoga teachers.

This brown-robed German nun was teaching Buddhist doctrines from scripture. She then talked about very basic meditation stuff – about posture, the breath, length of sittings.

Any questions?

People were asking about the management of pins and needles in their legs and I thought, 'sod it', and asked my question about going into a state of non-existence! I felt so stupid and pretentious, but I knew she knew.

"How long have you been meditating?" she barked in reply.

It was 12 years at the time.

"You should have experienced this before now!" She was so fierce. And that was that. No other comment, and onto the next question about toe cramps.

It was a lovely day, with walking meditation outside on the village green, dappled with sunshine and shaded by old oak trees. But I was none the wiser.

At the end, I was just going up to the organisers to thank them for their lovely day when a loud, uncompromising voice behind me said, "I have to teach this woman."

And that was me.

So we went to the organiser's house and sat in a little room with a cup of tea.

This dour nun asked what happened when I first sat down? What then? What then?

I was required to write them down.

And we eventually had a shopping list of my experiences, in the order that they happened, right up to the freaky one.

She said I had to buy a whopping book from the Buddhist Publication Society in Sri Lanka called the *Visuddhi Maggha* and read that, then come on retreat with her for ten days in a few months' time when she would be back in England, down in the south.

So I did.

The book – oh, what a relief, I can't tell you. It was repetitive and boring, as befits an aural, chanted transmission of knowledge, but it was all there.

Everything I had experienced was there and in exactly the same order that I had experienced it.

It was weird and amazing. How could this be?

It even spelled out the state of consciousness that had freaked me so utterly. It was 'the void' and it was fine. In fact there were more states to be experienced after that.

And it was all written down over 2,500 years ago.

I felt safe and reassured. I wasn't going mad.

Ayya Khema's words rang in my ears – "Nobody ever lost their personality, you can pick it up at the door on the way out!"

Turns out that these experiences were altered states of consciousness, noticed and codified by Buddhist monks all that time ago. I went on a retreat with Ayya Khema as suggested to experience them more fully.

With devastating results.

14

Retreat with scary nun

My devastating retreat with Ayya Khema was in fact magical. I was in the ghastliness of life after my marriage breakdown at the time. I cried for the first three days solid, not being able to run away and be distracted from my thoughts, structured meditation practice being the only game in town.

AK suddenly decided that she couldn't accept that I had gone spontaneously into the jhanas, or meditative absorptions. She said it wasn't possible without a teacher – maybe it was the sobbing.

We decided that I should go into one of the states each day, report to her every evening to debrief, then again every early morning to plot a course for the new day.

I did this and the meditative absorptions were experienced just as I experienced them after playschool, only here I was going deeper and deeper in.

I now understood that when a new state arose, you focused your attention solely on that and let any previous state go. You let this new state of consciousness become the object of your meditation. Because the states are so delightful it is a breeze to meditate for hours. It's exactly what you *want* to do.

I was chatting to AK one day and mentioned that I didn't know how all the other meditators in the hall did it – following the breath all day, just battling the mind without a glimpse of bliss, so difficult, so dry. She agreed with me and said she didn't know either.

Still, all that focus would work, it is a means to an end. I suppose I *had* put the work in before, only my way had been via devotion, to God with the BKs, or to my Guru, both of which practices were a delight, and so easy compared with the rigors and discipline of following the breath. But you need to learn sustained focus by some method, in order to bring your mind into one-pointedness.

Anyway, there I was with the states arising one after the other, in the right order, just like it said in the *Visuddhi Maggha*.

There are eight absorptions. And they arise spontaneously and unbidden if you get quiet enough in your meditation, or your life. It's just how it is.

THE MATERIAL ABSORPTIONS

The first four states of consciousness are called the material absorptions because they are closely associated with the body.

The first, bliss or rapture, is experience largely around the head. It's sparkling of course, and your one-pointed mind has no difficulty staying there – it has to beat the bloody breath doesn't it?

You do get insights in the bliss state. You realise that you have the power to experience bliss any time you want, with no input from the external world, and this can boost your confidence no end. It is all your own doing, and it is uncovering who you really are. Underneath that grime and grot you are bliss.

What a relief.

It also gives the lie to the common sentiment: 'You make me angry'. No, you do that to yourself. You could choose bliss in response to any slings and arrows of outrageous work colleague.

The second absorption to arise is emotional joy and you feel it in your chest, in your heart. It is as if your heart opens in gratitude for all the blissful stuff.

Bliss and joy often arise together, but joy is the more subtle and if you allow the mind to focus on joy it permeates the whole body from the heart.

The third is calmness, felt in the solar plexus. All your desires are satiated by the bliss and joy and there is nothing left to crave – so there is total calm and contentment.

The fourth is equanimity as the mind sinks further into peace and calm. This is usually associated with the abdomen and you can feel a softening and expansion of the abdomen. The equanimity is so soft, vast and profound. But it is amazingly dynamic and alive, not slothful or torpid. It is full and bright and there's nothing to do. All is complete.

I was having a great time experiencing all the states in such depth.

THE IMMATERIAL ABSORPTIONS

The fifth state was lovely, it's called the base of boundless space. It is lightness and spaciousness, and it's limitless. You are not in your body anymore, you are expanded spaciousness.

Then comes the sixth, the base of boundless consciousness. It's still vast, but the space is conscious. There is thrilling spacious joy and unity. It is as if at this level there is only one of us here. All things, every blade of grass or spiral nebula are one, one consciousness.

The seventh is the void, which so shocked me at first. It's just empty, gone. Nowhere to stand. But then, nothing exists to stand anywhere anyway.

At this point you still *are*. Not to panic. You are still a 'you' because *you* are aware of the state. You still exist or at least, you don't, but you *know* that you don't, so you're still there busy knowing, observing the non-existence of everything, including you.

Going now into the eighth *jhana*, the base of neither perception nor non-perception. That knowing we had in the void, that individual consciousness gets more shaky here.

The mind is jacking it in, giving up the struggle. It is content to be still, not discriminating, choosing, or judging. Things are and they are not.

STREAM ENTRY

Following on from this, the mind does give up, the ego throws in the towel and in my case, for one brief moment I didn't exist. It was shocking, completely shocking.

AK saw me in the corridor and led me to her room, bewildered. I had just experienced a sort of internal pop, a hiatus in existence, almost impossible to explain. AK said I had to meditate on it all night – which was OK as you don't need much sleep when the mind is so quiet.

I saw her in the morning.

Sorry to say, that only the day before I had been arguing the toss with AK in her morning class about a point of scripture (I was going down fighting) and here I was the next day, after the 'pop' experience, and AK asked me, "What do you think of the teaching of the Buddha now?"

Shockingly, this voice, which didn't sound like me, it was authoritative and solid, came out of me and said, "I have no doubt."

I think I was more surprised than she was. She just said, "That's Stream Entry."

She was dismissive as usual and said I had experienced it all without a teacher, "because of the imprint of past lives."

No big deal then.

But Stream Entry is mind-blowing, literally. It's direct knowing, where you don't exist anymore, and *It Is*.

You know.

You've experienced the truth for yourself. You can't be taught any more, because you know. You've seen through the game.

I mean it's only the first level of enlightenment, but still, it changed everything.

AK said, "You have to take the robes now." (Become a nun).

"No, I'm not going to do that," I said, "because I still enjoy a gin and tonic". (My metaphor for all this stuff, people, society.)

She surprised me by accepting this, telling me to keep in touch with her and to go on lots of retreats. But even with a matter of fact approach, it still took a long time to readjust to 'normal' life, and it's never seemed quite real since.

So that's me. I've seen momentarily through the game, but I still have all my 'defilements' – anger (as you've seen), hatred, ill-will, sloth, torpor etc...

Only now, they all seem unnecessary and a bit of a giggle really – 'Oh, there's that crossness again'.

I mean, why covet your neighbour's ox when you and your neighbour are one, and so is the ox, come to that.

It's like the right hand being jealous of the ring on the left hand. Bonkers.

They say that, having seen through the game, the defilements created by illusion fall away – because they're so pointless presumably.

I'm still waiting.

MONKS' ISLAND

Some time later, I was going to Sri Lanka on holiday with my present husband. I thought it was

174

a great opportunity to visit the jungle island where AK practiced, and later to visit the Venerable Nyanaponika at his forest hermitage before he died. He was in his nineties.

I had a postcard with a Buddha on the front from AK, who was in Germany, giving me the address of *Nun's* Island, but with the injunction to give them a month's notice of any visit.

I was going in two weeks!

We found our way by 'tuk-tuk' to the lake, but couldn't find a launch jetty. We did come across three local lads who would take us out to Nun's Island paddling a dug out tree with the roots still attached.

Well, you had to didn't you?!

One of them had a monkey on his shoulder.

It took hours, in the boiling sun, with beautiful, bright turquoise kingfishers swooping around us.

The boys were suddenly scared witless as we approached Nun's Island. It had big, threatening, Keep Out notices by the jetty. In fact, it turned out to be closed for refurbishment! A lovely caretaker nun directed me to neighbouring Monk's Island for a dharma talk.

They were lovely on Monk's Island it was a magical atmosphere, my postcard was passed around and much venerated. They fed us and gave us coconut water to drink. They were very nurturing and very protective of me.

I found myself sitting enraptured before this wonderful old monk who, straight away, asked me: "When you meditate, are you there?"

I knew exactly what he meant.

He was asking if I'd had Stream Entry.

Can you tell me why, when it had been the most extraordinary defining moment of my life, in front of this wonderful man, I lied.

I said yes, I am there.

I was so overcome by the moment and his powerful simplicity that I considered my paltry moment of Stream Entry absolutely too pathetic to bring before him. I mean, he was living it – and I'd had a 'pop' experience. It felt too silly.

Too silly? I'm still kicking myself.

I was in some sort of loved-up trance and altered state and he seemed to know anyway. But what a conversation might we have had, what wisdom, what lightness, what pointers could he have shared?

My nun's view was typically pragmatic. "You've got this far without a teacher, you can do the rest!"

What rest?

15

Intention and
car parking spaces

When teaching meditation I found to my delight that there were one or two people who could go into some of the jhanas (altered states of consciousness). The bar of required concentration was too high for most though.

How could I help more people experience their higher potential, these altered states?

This is where intention comes in.

We've already seen that intention can affect the decay of a radioactive isotope, and just *noticing* an experiment affects the results of that experiment.

So your mind and intentions matter.

What if you *intended* to experience those wonderful altered states, like bliss, or joy? I mean, just those first two jhanas would keep you going for a lifetime wouldn't they?

The experience of bliss and joy *at will*, would give a huge boost to your inner confidence, giving a much more relaxed attitude to the old day to day.

THE LAW OF ATTRACTION

I feel I ought to explain about the law of attraction, it has been very popular and is all about intending, on a material level.

The idea behind the law of attraction is that you get what you intend, what you want. So you'd think the results would be obvious for all to see – we spend most of our lives intending and wanting after all. OK so if there is this law, why are we not manifesting all our thoughts and desires out there in the world, right now?

The reason the law of attraction is not obvious is because our thoughts are not laser sharp and focused. Most people's thoughts are scattered and contradictory, chaotic. Chaotic thinking would produce a chaotic world. No, surely not.

Obviously, if we had honed our minds into wonderful extensions of our will *and* learned to come into the moment, the world would be ours, we would be able to manifest like nobody's business. But it's a bit like Christ's – if you had but faith you could move mountains – the trouble is, if you had that degree of faith, or surrender into the Oneness, you would be the Enlightened One and remember why you put the mountain there in the first place. So why would you move it?

But with a moderate amount of focus we *can* experience intending and getting, in our everyday, material world. They call it Cosmic Ordering.

Such a pity that it seems mostly to be in the form of intending a Caribbean holiday or a sizzling new kitchen appliance.

Before I get on my high horse about this intending though, I did it recently when I wanted to quickly nip down to the Post Office in the local town, but needed to park nearby as I didn't have much time. I vividly imagined an empty space and easy parking.

(Obviously I'd love to say that I'd used my mind and intention to help create world peace, but no, it was a parking space close to the Post Office.)

Still, it was encouraging, because at 11am, the busiest time of the day, I was almost embarrassed to see that there were huge spaces to park, all over the place. I only needed one!

I slipped into a space big enough for a tank right outside the PO. Feeling guilty.

Strangely, when I came out later and drove off I noticed that all the spaces were taken and the town was full.

That's it, intending, at the rather manipulative macro level. Which is fine, everything is grist for our mill and a learning opportunity. It's not wrong, but it's more interesting at, and really has its roots in, the micro level of our energy systems and we will go on to experience this later.

LASSOING THE LAW OF ATTRACTION

We'll explore the law of attraction first then see if we can use it for spiritual purposes.

The story of the law is that in order for the Universe to give you what you want on the level of material things, you have to be *focused* and imagine *your wish already fulfilled*. The *desired outcome* is then in your mind. You are intending it.

If you really want something you need to imagine you *have it already*, in every detail, using all your senses. Then you will attract that thing to you. Hence – the law of attraction.

You sort of attract what you are, what your thoughts are.

So you want the new car? Don't leave it at that, don't simply keep wanting, or you will just attract more wanting. You'll never get the car. Because you are thinking *wanting*.

Imagine that you *have* the car already, the make, the colour, the smell of the leather, the performance, the sound of the engine, the clunk of the door shutting, what it feels like to drive. Feel *grateful,* as you would if it were already yours. Then the Universe can't help but give it to you.

You can imagine it intensely a few times a day. Make it a practice. Don't let it slide. (All very exhausting, and you'll go off the car once you get it, but don't believe me, for the sake of this experiment, persevere.)

Put pictures around the house or office where you will see them.

You just need to pay attention each time you look at the pictures and stay in the moment, you have that car in the infinite present.

And then, when you *do* get the car, don't shrug it off as coincidence, write it down.

Notice the timing.

To recap, getting what you want as soon as you intend it would be a miracle, like being a spiritual magician. But mostly there is a time delay between intending and the thing happening. So notice it.

We're talking synchronicity, a miracle on a timer.

However, you may find that *surrender,* to the universe, to God, works amazingly well too, try it and see. Larry Dossey had groups of people all over America praying for germinating trays of seeds with specific prayers, and 'Thy will be done' worked the best. (They grew even better than the 'Love' or 'Gratitude' ones.)

AWARENESS AND INTENTION

OK, so now let's get down with pure energy, where the fun begins.

First we need to get to grips with the idea of the Oneness. We could think of the Oneness as being all-pervading Consciousness or Awareness. Infinite Awareness. It is in everything, it *is* everything. It is us, what we are made of, and we are part of *it*. So everything is connected through it.

It knows what we are thinking because it is who we are, as is everything else. We are in a symbiotic dance with ourselves, with this Infinite Awareness. The dance is the dance of life.

Because infinite *anything* is beyond our imagining we can make Infinite Awareness more user-friendly if we use the terms 'Sea of Consciousness', 'Sea of Awareness', or 'Ocean of Awareness'. We can just about imagine an ocean, though it's still pretty big to us.

In the exercise that is to follow we can see for ourselves how our *individual* awareness or consciousness is linked to the Infinite Awareness, or Sea of Awareness.

The idea is that when we close our eyes and tune in to the individual energy system that is us, we get a real feel for what is going on inside.

With our eyes closed the body doesn't feel solid, it all feels like energy anyway.

We can calm down a little first, perhaps following the breath for a few minutes to help the process. Notice how your body really does just feel like energy with your eyes closed and that you can even tell that the energy is a little calmer now for focusing on the breath. You can discern changes in the energy.

Then you can hold an intention in your mind and see what happens.

You hold an intention to experience Love or Joy, or perhaps Fear, and you can *instantly* notice a difference in your energy system. It's surprising. (Check out Jeddah Mali who does great work on this).

It is as if your consciousness becomes more expansive, it *meshes* with the Sea of Awareness and the Awareness reflects back to you what you're putting out. You can see how deliberate intending works on you, on your energy system. Also it's how vibrant good health would be easy if your thinking were healthy, and, who knows, ill health may well follow from negative thoughts like habitual anger or inveterate fearfulness.

You notice that the positive emotions you intend feel light, expansive and lovely in your energy system and the negative ones feel contracted and heavy and horrible. Good to know that.

Remember, you can choose what you think and what you believe.

Your thinking affects your energy system or energy body. And at a fundamental level you *are* your energy body, the material body is a reflection of that energetic blueprint.

So your thinking makes your body.

Not only that, your energy body gives you experience and really, your life is the totality of your experiences.

We need to look after our energy body, so we need to look after our thinking.

What happens in effect is that our thoughts produce changes and distortions in our energy system, we will experience that, and if the thoughts are persistent and habitual enough these distortions then materialise in physical form, and we certainly experience that. Persistent anger would upset your energy system and quite likely lead to high blood pressure and a pugnacious expression.

Those habitual thoughts thus become visible to the world, say, the down-turned mouth and frown lines – they show, they tell a story. Maybe they are from the contracting effects of long term anxiety and worry, playing havoc with the flow of your *qi*, which would then affect your internal organs as well, making you out of balance and eventually unwell.

The good news is that we don't have to keep thoughts we don't want. Just like we said earlier in Mindfulness, our negative thoughts are not the truth, even those that say they are. And those negative thoughts are not serving us well.

When we hold an intention or thought and the Awareness mirrors it back to us, it is a biofeedback device.

The Oneness constantly and consistently mirrors back to us our thoughts, and we experience things.

So how are we doing so far? If the world is in a mess, our thinking must be in a mess.

Once we get the hang of it though we can get into an upward rather than a downward spiral. Beautiful thoughts register as beautiful feelings and we are *grateful*, thereby producing *more* beautiful feelings, because gratitude is so very powerful and positive.

We notice when negative thoughts creep in because we lose our spaciousness and lightness, we become heavy, tight and unhappy. This becomes our experience.

Now that we know the mechanisms, can we change our thinking to change ourselves, and our moods? We can have a go. Not by *pretending* to be positive, but if we meditate regularly and get in touch with our expansive, loving, true self – that's automatically positive. And as our positive energy spreads out into the world, we are also changing the world into a more positive and loving place. By osmosis.

Too good to be true? Who knows? But it can't hurt anyone and could be a great experiment.

Go round the supermarket when you are in love and it's a delightful place, people smile at you and chat about veg and stuff. Someone bumps into you with their trolley and you smile and say that you can't drive yours either, you feel like buddies. The checkout queue is populated by friends or potential friends.

Go round the same supermarket when you're angry and it's grim. People barge into your ankles and don't care, and you end up wanting to kill and forgetting half of your list.

Good to know that we are taking care of this thinking business, isn't it?

16

A contemplation on Awareness and Intention

Right, so you have the amazing ability to use intention to affect the material world, out there, and I am suggesting that you can change your internal landscape to experience, say, joy.

This way you get instant feedback, not just a new car three months down the line, which would be put down to coincidence and a fortuitous tax rebate anyway.

Well hold onto your hat Dorothy.

Let's get some biofeedback and see how this stuff really works.

You need to be present – in the Now – but a simple focus on the breath, and then the body, will take care of that.

Then there is acceptance (or at least a suspension of your disbelief) that there is a force which permeates all things, we are calling it the Sea of Awareness, but you could call it Nigel if you wanted. It is Infinite Consciousness, Infinite Awareness, the Oneness.

It might take a few attempts to tune into what you feel like inside, but keep going, it's easy, and you will notice how the inside changes with your intentions. You will experience the changes.

All set?

HOLDING INTENTIONS: A CONTEMPLATION

As with any contemplation, you could read the following, then do the contemplation with the odd peek at the words to remind yourself; record them and play it back; or maybe get a friend to read the words to you. The words need to be read very slowly, with big pauses.

First, sit quietly in a chair with your feet firmly on the floor, and your hands loosely in your lap, palms up or down. Try not to cross the arms, lace the fingers or cross the legs, these are all 'defensive' postures and we are trying to be relaxed and open. Or of course, you can sit cross-legged on a cushion on the floor, looking cool, but again don't fold your arms or lace your fingers.

Gently close your eyes, take a few deep breaths and with each long and delicious out-breath allow the shoulders to relax, soften and drop a little.

Breathing normally now, soften and relax the back of your neck, drop the chin a little and extend the neck, create space below the head. In Chinese medicine there is a 'window on heaven' point there. Give the window some space. Taoists would start by massaging just there to facilitate meditation.

Become aware of your relaxed breathing.

The breath is in the present moment, so already you are coming into the Now. Begin to feel that the slow breath, and the focus on it, is easing in a feeling of calm and relaxation. Inviting it.

Nowhere to go.

Just be here.

Scan your body. How you are feeling? Any tension or discomfort? Just acknowledge the feelings, allow them. Soften again and let them go. You can pick them up later if you need to.

Just a gentle awareness on the breath. A letting go.

You are in the moment, relaxed. Your consciousness is part of the Universal Consciousness, the Ocean of Awareness, this vast sea of creativity, of wellbeing and love. You are immersed in it.

You can access this Sea of Awareness in the present moment.

You are going to use your consciousness to create an intention and see what the Sea of Awareness does with it. You will notice whether you can feel changes in your experience of yourself, whether the Awareness responds to you.

First notice that with the eyes closed the body is experienced as energy. Feel it. Notice the quality of your energy system. Is it jangled, or congested, or smooth? Just notice how it is.

Now, you are going to use your conscious mind to intend, to create an intention.

Say to yourself: 'I am going to hold an intention to experience Love.'

You are aware of your body energy system as you hold the intention. Just see what happens in that energy system. See if it changes. Notice any changes.

Notice.

Just the intention to experience love. It is a really clear intention for the Sea of Awareness.

For me, when I hold the intention to experience love, and I focus on my body, I get a tingling where my solar plexus would be if I had my eyes open. It's a light, tingling sensation, expansive as if this lovely feeling, were spreading up and out from my solar plexus. Where my ribs diverge feels soft and excited and that feeling comes out from the body. Upwards and outwards. It is subtle, but nice.

Delightful.

Your experience in response to this intention may be different. Just focus and notice, in this moment, how does it feel to hold an intention to experience love? What does love feel like? Does your energy system change to a new pattern that you recognise as love?

Sit with that for a while. Notice that the more you focus on the word 'Love', or on the feeling it gives you, the more the experience of love grows. You do in fact recognise the feeling as love without having to consciously manufacture it.

Don't worry if you are not tuned in to the experiences yet, they are subtle and it soon gets easier.

So that was Love, the intention of experiencing love. Now we will change the intention.

We are going to hold an intention to experience Peace.

Intend Peace.

How does your body feel? Is there a different quality to the feeling in your energy body when you focus on experiencing peace?

When I intend to experience peace I get a more outward feeling as if my chest and solar plexus were expanding. It's light, delightful, expansive and delicious, as if my ribs at the sides were expanding and there is a sweet feeling in my chest and throat.

And, what is simply gobsmacking is that the feeling comes *immediately*, there is no delay. As soon as I intend to experience peace, there it is. Peace, with all these expansive feelings, such texture and depth.

Notice for yourself, can you feel a change?

The Sea of Awareness is the medium of our existence. We exist in it, and it permeates through us.

There is no space between it and us. It is who we are.

It is the mirror for our intentions, and because we are totally in the moment, when we hold the intention to experience peace, we notice the experience immediately. Remember, a synchronicity experienced with no time delay is called a miracle, and it does feel pretty miraculous and quite unexpected. Shocking almost.

And all we've done is focus and intend.

Feel it for yourself.

Focus.

What does it feel like when you intend peace? Experience your energy body, become aware of the changes and the absolute immediacy of the changes. Notice.

Also notice that as you continue to focus on peace, either the word peace itself or the feelings of peace, the sensations in your energy system grow, they intensify with your intention. It is quite delightful.

And it hasn't depended on someone being nice to you. We haven't had to fix your life, sort out your relationships.

Wonderful peace. Freely available.

After sitting in peace for a while, change the intention. 'I am going to hold an intention to experience – compassion.'

What's that one like?

Again immediately there is an experience. Notice it. For me it is as if energy is streaming out of my heart in front of me and going outwards and upwards, very sweet. What about you? Notice the change and notice the immediacy of the change.

Hold an intention to experience joy.

The Sea of Awareness cannot help but respond to your intention in the Now. The Awareness *is* you, and you are it. In the Now there are no barriers between you and the Awareness.

I am holding an intention to experience joy – magic, here it is. For me I feel it straight away, it's as if there is a vortex of energy coming from my solar plexus or my heart, going up and out. My head seems to soften and expand into comfortable, light-expanding, thrilling joy.

It's immediate, like putting in my order and the waitress producing my desire from behind her back saying: "Voila!"

Notice.

It is as if the Universe is saying, "You want to know what peace feels like – it feels like this. You want to know what joy feels like – it feels like this."

Notice it. They didn't call the Buddha the Awakened One for nothing. He noticed. We need to wake up and experience what happens in our consciousness and in our energy systems. There is no blind belief here, notice that as you focus on one state, it increases. More and more.

What about thinking, what effect does that have? We can hold a thought, 'I am lovely.' There may be resistance and you may think it false or, if you are in fact drop-dead gorgeous, it may feel narcissistic to think it. However, it's OK, who you are is the Oneness, and It is lovely, so you can go with it.

I am lovely.

Feel the changes, expansive, giggly and delightful. Enjoy the experience.

OK, now what about fear? That's very familiar in our lives.

If we think about fear what happens?

For me, just thinking, or considering thinking, about fear contracts my stomach, my solar plexus. It is as if my lower ribs and my stomach are drawing in, tensing.

Notice for you.

This is often the first experience people notice in this contemplation, it is so powerful.

Notice any tightening, drawing in.

This tells us so much. Fear is contracting, it is making us *less than* who we are. Fear is not our original nature, the nature of the Oneness itself, it can't be, it diminishes us and makes us small and cramped. There is no way the Oneness is small and cramped. It's infinite, for God's sake.

So fear diminishes us, it makes us 'less than'.

Give yourself a break and hold the intention to experience joy again.

Notice the immediacy of the change, the expansion. Staying with the intention to experience joy. Delightfully, the solar plexus instantly softens, the more I intend, the ribs become more expansive, the whorl of energy expands around my heart and my head, going up and up. So different. Harmonious, wonderful.

What we notice is that positive states of, say, love, compassion, peace or joy make us 'more than'. They are expansive, light and delightful. They are the ones that are in tune with our original nature, the nature of the Sea of Awareness, the force of the universe – who we really are.

Notice it all. Focus your consciousness.

Fully experience. Just rest in joy, feel deep gratitude for the Sea of Awareness, this matrix, giving us whatever experience we intend, instantly. Feel the positive power that this gives us in our lives. Be impressed by the power of your consciousness and the immediacy of its effects.

Notice the inevitability of experience following intention.

All we are at the level of human beings is a set of experiences, our lives *are* our experiences – and all we experience is our intending.

We suddenly realise that this is all that has ever happened, we have had thoughts and intentions and the universe has given us the experience, immediately. But we never noticed. We were too sucked into the drama and business.

So if you have a life full of fear and anger, hatred and fights, you know what your habitual thoughts and intentions are. They are fearful and angry.

If you have a confused mess of vacillating states in your life, you know what a confused mess of vacillating thoughts and intentions you have.

Great.

Good to know. Knowledge is power, we have the power now to do something about it. We can come into the moment and intend more positive states.

Next time you are feeling anxious and depressed, you could say, 'I intend to experience peace'. And you will if you focus on your body. If you come into the moment, you have to. As you've noticed, it is an immediate and mandatory response, inevitable. Peace becomes inevitable.

Expand into peace now. The real power of intention.

Enjoy.

Now allow your consciousness to come back into your body, the room, your life. With your eyes still closed, smile, and feel the smile light up all the cells in your body.

Deepen your breathing slightly, move your fingers and toes, returning to normal waking consciousness.

If anxiety instantly assails you the moment you pick up the reins, realise that this is bad attack of future thoughts, so just substitute 'I could be experiencing peace instead of this,' or, 'Do I really have to worry about this, I could be peaceful?' Make a long exhalation to stimulate the vagus nerve and trigger the relaxation response. Allow your stomach and chest to relax, you can come back to this instant, now, and peace.

And the experience of substituting a positive state for a negative state, a thought you want for one you don't want, gives you such confidence, no matter what life has in store, you can always intend peace.

BACK TO ME (ME, ME):

I was in the car with my husband driving and he was getting cross with other drivers, the weather, everything. He was just cross. Easy for me to be calm, I wasn't driving. But his anger was uncomfortable to be around and I was finding it draining as I couldn't escape.

Then I made the mental decision to stop judging him, and instead I allowed myself to understand, the stresses of his life, the fear that other drivers were a danger. I held an intention to experience love. My solar plexus was tingling and soft and the more I focused on love, the more the feeling grew. There was love to spare, spilling over into the car, the neighbourhoods through which we drove.

The next remark my husband made, some minutes later, was silly, good-natured and very funny. He felt the love, the fear just went away.

We are all connected. I can't change him, or anyone else, only myself. But if I change, then my world changes. It's amazing to think that we have that skill, and that choice.

So can the knowledge of the power of our minds really help in a rather bleak world? I think it can, because the world is not quite as immutable, as rigid, as it seems.

17

A yawning chasm in reality – help!

The negative stuff we do that complicates our lives and makes our drama so juicy, ghastly and absorbing comes from our fear.

What fear?

There *is* something, that is largely ignored, and *scary*.

And of course when we are scared, we contract, as we have experienced in the last chapter. We feel small, alone and frightened. That's when we may get angry, defend ourselves by attack, and are likely to lash out. And that's just what we do. That's life as we experience it.

So what is the scary thing that we are ignoring?

It's this:

We don't know who we are, we don't know where we came from, we don't know where we will go when we die and we don't have a clue what it is all for.

This constitutes a gaping chasm in our version of life. But we are nothing if not inventive, and we cover it up. We are surprised when the hole is brought to our attention.

Mostly we ignore it and keep busy so as not to have to consider such things, but we know it's there, which makes us uneasy.

I mean, let's face it, I'm a fragile life-form on a cooling rock hurtling through space, dependent on a decaying sun and cooperation from the rest of my species for survival. The rest of my species are not known for their altruism, nor even for having the sense they were born with. As we speak they are hacking away at, and polluting, the habitat in which we stand – oh, and killing each other.

And I don't even know what I am.

Still, what's for tea? If I get a move on I could fit in a session at the gym before supper.

It seems to me that inner enquiry would be the answer. However I'm always getting side-tracked by the seductiveness of my life or I get lost in the picky details of meditation practice: the how to or where to, or the guilt of not having practiced for weeks on end.

So what's the point?

I meet earnest spiritual seekers and feel no affinity for them feeling their forced external calm and inner turmoil, I meet city slickers lost in their latest electronic devices and material wealth, and don't get that either.

But, for goodness sake, *they're* not sitting with scorpions on their heads are they? So who's better off? What am I doing this for? I have to go deeper.

Is the world as it appears or are there deeper games afoot? I've been suggesting ways of becoming quiet and looking inside for truth about what's going on, to open our eyes and see clearly. That sounds reasonable, but why do we need to do that? What are we doing the rest of the time?

We seem to be selecting the reality we want.

We are good at make-believe. For a start our eyes see the world upside down so we put that right; and we should see the world with two holes in it, one for each eye. There is a hole in the retina of each eye where the optic nerve enters the eye. We don't see two holes, we invent more of what we are seeing and so see a continuous whole.

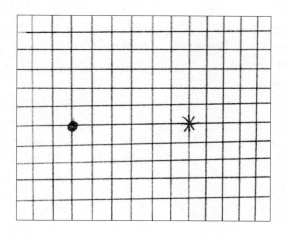

Look at the diagram of the grid, there is a dot on the left and a star on the right. Hold the page up in front of you so that it is more or less level with your nose. Now close your right eye and look at the star shape on the right of the grid. You can still see the dot on the left in your peripheral vision. Very slowly move the diagram closer in and then further away from you. You will notice that there is a point where the dot disappears. This is because the light coming from the dot is falling on the point on your left retina where the optic nerve enters the eye.

The interesting thing is that as it disappears, the grid appears continuous where the dot should be. The mind made it up, it made it look as if the dot was never there at all.

We make things up and we ignore stuff that doesn't fit, and we stick to our story. For instance, there are *billions* of bits of available sensory data bombarding us right now, we live in tons of it, like an information soup, we ignore it all. There are cosmic rays passing straight through you as you read this and then on through the Earth and out the other side, they are not important to you, they don't add to your story, so you ignore them.

We sift through information and narrow it down to what we accept as reality, and bypass the overwhelming mass of it. We have a socially conditioned idea of what is 'normal' and the way we construct our world is to reject anything that doesn't fit in with that paradigm.

You have a need to make everything make sense, but would never *believe* that you make it up. You trust your senses – big mistake. Turns out, your senses are selective, giving you the illusion of continuity, stability, safety.

Life is patently *not* stable. But we actually get cross and think it unfair when things go wrong in our little lives, as if we have a life rule book that says: if I'm good and pay my taxes I won't get cancer; if I'm good and recycle my rubbish I won't get run over. And when stuff happens, we think it is a big mistake and an injustice.

And what about the truth about who am I? What will happen to me when I die and who started all this? That black hole at the centre of our lives, what about that?

Confronted with these questions, we usually *go to sleep* into our mellow drama and kill time until we die anyway, filling our lives with triumphs and disasters, too busy to think and deciding that all this is enough. A good life. Until, that is, we are on our deathbeds, are diagnosed with mortal illness, or have a milestone birthday of 50/60/70, when we ask, "What was that about?" or, "There has to be more to life than this."

Usually we manage to extract our heads from the sand enough to rely on the *investigations done by others*. We almost look at the chasm, we sort of take a sideways glance.

This is often when we plump for some religion or other. The religion then tells us a story about what happened to cause it all, why, and what will happen when we die.

Phew, that was close, we don't have to think about that any more, it's taken care of.

Only there are still huge flaws in the logic if we look closely, and it begs the question of how do *they* know? But if you question it you are a heretic and get thrown off the team.

What to do? Often you decide that compliance and profound belief seem a price well worth paying to keep you in the religion, which gives you the security of the group. Of course it's best not to think about it too much in case you find a hiccup in the detail. But, wait, better yet, you can become a hero, admired in the group, by becoming really zealous. You can close your mind to reason or other paths except for the teachings of your chosen religion.

You'll get great admiration and support from the other team members.

OPENING THE MIND

There is a third course open to you when confronted by the elephant in the cosmic room. So far we have considered snoozing through life and blind faith.

You could always *investigate*. Search for truth yourself. It is a metaphysical truth we are after. OK, it's a bit heavy for the pub quiz, but people do it, it's not just you. The internet is awash with exotic retreats in lovely places where you can begin to become more introspective. Or there are Buddhist one's with more rigor.

Truth, as opposed to faith, requires an open mind, ruthlessly open, with the courage to go outside the norm – and a whopping sense of humour.

The delight in this approach is that, with an open mind, when someone disagrees with you, you are *grateful* for it. Imagine. You value the observation, you take it on board and evaluate it, turn it around and see if it fits, see if it has value, more value than your original idea maybe.

WHERE FEAR COMES IN

If you have a belief, it is not your *truth* it is a *belief*. You believe what you have been told. You are not questioning, not looking. You are not seeking the truth, you believe that what you have been told *is* the truth. This closes your mind.

If someone then comes along with an alternative explanation for the elephant in the room, their alternative explanation has to be *resisted* because it threatens to be more realistic or seductive than your belief. If you take their explanation on board, then you may lose your belief and feel cut adrift without the prop of your faith and your religious mates. Disaster.

Worse still, you could be thrown out of the team with dire warnings of damnation. Don't get me wrong, a belief handed down to you by some huge authoritative system is great, it can be very comforting. A system of belief can give you a moral compass, companionship of the group and even a career with the prospect of rising through the ranks to chief canonical text bearer. And think of the frocks! Then there's beards, hats, silks, staffs – it's all terrific. And it could be your path for a while, we've all had many paths and they have given us many gifts.

But does it have the monopoly on truth? Is it the only way?

The original holy man of a religion was doubtless wonderful, he had the enlightenment experience, lived his life simply, in the Oneness, with his feet barely on the Earth and was a great example to us all of what could be done if we were to do like him and surrender to the Oneness ourselves.

Unfortunately, we try to surrender to the holy man, and not the Oneness. We mistake the messenger for the message. But even his message is only *his* message, his version of truth.

Truth is so massive that we cannot conceive of it and once glimpsed we cannot recount it except by allusion and metaphor. In effect the wonderful holy person is telling of the Oneness as he experienced it. The infinite system, the Oneness, Source, is mediated through a little system, this human, giving us enlightened-sage-flavoured-Oneness.

And even then, his method of getting to God may have been perfect for him, but it may not be your way through at all.

It gets worse, because our wonderful enlightened sage, in touch with the Cosmos, producing his concomitant and inevitable miracles – acquires *disciples*. The disciples write it all down, or world leaders adopt the now deceased sage and write down a version of his story that suits them. Then not only are the teachings not necessarily applicable to us individually as a path to enlightenment, they get subtly, or not so subtly, changed to give power to the people running the show.

This is the religion that has sprung up to take advantage of the teaching and fill the void in our lives.

Trouble is it doesn't even end *there*. If you are so frightened by the management into believing that this is right and in fact *only* this is right, that makes everyone else outside your religion *wrong*. You have to become intolerant, either mildly or even violently of other people's paths. The others are obviously misguided but worse, a danger. They are a danger because they could tempt your members off the true path.

An awful lot of wars are fought in the name of religion.

It's true of any big organisation: we are weak and puny as individuals and powerful in a group. Let's fight for the group, it's a tribal thing. Let's then convert the vanquished when we win, getting more converts and a bigger group. It just shows our truth is the greatest.

Our fears are allayed. Oh and of course, we must have had God on our side.

OK THAT'S FEAR, HOW WOULD IT BE WITH LOVE?

If aggro comes from fear, tolerance comes from love.

"Brilliant that you have found a way through, I am seeking my way through too, how's it hanging?"

Beyond all differences we are all the Oneness. There is so much more that unites us than divides us. Recognition of that unity is a wonderful start.

We are all, in effect, on a journey to *nothingness* (no ego) or put another way, *everything* (the infinite whole) beyond the illusions of form and thought.

The 'end' of the journey is expansive and limitless and is the same for all of us and it always was.

Don't be put off by any of this, the journey, your curriculum, is as peaceful as the degree to which you surrender to it. You can do it kicking and screaming or with delicious surrender into the truth, but the journey is satisfying, as nothing else can be

And if your questioning has been awoken, but not satisfied by my skilfully crafted rants, are there other methods?

You betcha!

18

I can't do any of that!
How else can I get there?

This journey back to Source, isn't a linear journey. You are not at point A travelling to point B. You eventually discover that you are, in fact, point A and point B at the same time. You have been the Oneness, God, all the time. You're all of it.

God in drag, that's you.

We are trying so hard to open to limitless love, to become balanced and free. Or else trying to get pregnant, become the CEO of the group, or rob a bank. But if we could only let go, surrender into this moment completely, here we are, and were all the time, job done. For some of us the veil between the mundane us we're used to, and the gorgeous limitless version, is very thin. What to do?

What excites me is both the simplicity and the enormity of the predicament. We're talking about the transformation of us, from humans with the odd glimpse of spirituality, to spiritual beings consciously and compassionately being in our clever human form, free to explore this wonderful world we have created as our playground, with all the fear sucked out.

We have all that we need to experience limitlessness. We have the awareness of what feels good and bad, so we can learn. Our bodies are the best biofeedback-device ever, plus we have this astonishing biochemistry that can make a war, a baby and digest rhubarb at the same time. And now we have loads of ways through from the prosaic to a more cosmic consciousness.

But I'm still here, you say, sitting on my bottom with my ingrowing toenail giving me gyp.

So if reading the odd chapter hasn't made an enlightened being of you (what's the matter with you – honestly!) where else would it be helpful to go?

Clearly we do have to honour our physical form, the ingrowing toenail stuff. We have to look after our bodies, pay attention to them, eat well, sleep well and so on. It's hard to be light-filled with gout. These bodies are part of the plan, we register our emotional and spiritual states in them. Conversely, our physiology, the gout, the ingrowing and all the rest, affects our mental and emotional state.

A balanced body would be a peaceful platform to start with, that's what the practice of yoga is all about. But equally, an unbalanced body can give you the impetus and the juice to seek other ways in. ('Oh God this is intolerable. What am I doing wrong? What's life about? There has to be some point!' You know the thing.)

And there are, indeed, so many ways in. The wonderful Byron Katie for instance is saying: question your thinking. It's only believing your negative thoughts that upsets you, not the other people or circumstances in your life.

Which would be right when you think that the world is just a projection of your thoughts and emotions and the Oneness is always giving you the experiences you're asking for with your thoughts and intentions. So sort out your thinking.

Speaking of which, check out Jeddah Mali who does a lovely audio set called *The Seeds of Enlightenment*, she is right on the nail for how your intentions affect the Oneness and the feedback of the Oneness, immediately giving you the experience of your intention, your thought, because it has to, because it is you and you are it.

Dr David Hamilton writes lovely books on the power of the mind to affect the body, that mind–body connection.

I adore the first few lessons of the 'workbook' of *A Course in Miracles,* all about nothing being real or having inherent meaning (don't be put off by the main book, it has a very different feel to me).

Lesson one of the workbook starts with: *Nothing I see means anything.*

Lesson two: *I have given everything I see all the meaning that it has for me.*

How cool is that?

Then have a look at the wonderful poem: 'The Third Patriarch of Zen', all about choiceless awareness:

> *The Great Way is not difficult*
> *for those who have no preferences.*
> *When not attached to love or hate,*
> *all is clear and undisguised.*

It goes on in this vein, well, it's Zen, it was always going to be a bit fierce, but wonderful, you can look for the full text on line.

It ends with:

> *Words! Words!*
> *The Way is beyond language,*
> *for in it there is no yesterday,*
> *no tomorrow*
> *no today.*

So all of this was a bit of a waste of time then.

Yoga is toning and relaxing, a real treat for your body and gives you the beginnings of a meditative approach.

Pilates will tone the body and will give you a controlled workout.

A physical approach to check out is Network Spinal Analysis (NSA) and its sister therapy Somato Respiratory Integration (SRI) with Donny Epstein. SRI is about feeling and honouring the emotions within the body and has some parallels with Mindfulness. NSA is an energetic extension of chiropractic where ridiculously light touch on the top and base of the spine causes *qi* to flow and spirit to reconnect, forming a bridge between heaven and earth. It's an amazing spiritual rush, oh, and your back gets better too.

And speaking of bridges between heaven and earth, that's exactly what Acupuncturists are saying too. (Look at Lonny Jarrett's work if you've a mind to, though being an acupuncturist, and knowing the location of the points he's talking about, helps in the enjoyment.)

New physics is on the side of the angels, try *The Dancing Wu Li Masters* by Gary Zukav, or the many books by Marcus Chown.

It's all there and it's all the same in essence, because there's nowhere else to go, these are fundamental truths.

In the end all roads lead to this. There is nothing but love, nothing but God. So that makes you love and God (heavily disguised, admittedly).

Don't get precious about it, be honest, never pretend and speak in hushed tones to get that rarefied spiritual effect. Go for it, make the mistakes, fall flat on your face, pick yourself up, smile wryly at God and do it again, it's an endless trip to eternity, relax.

Stop when you are walking in countryside, really see that tree, shout "Yes" as you feel the enormity of the sensations and don't care who hears you. (Then look round, embarrassed, and pick up some litter, whistling gently.)

This is your wonderful life. There is Divinity and humanity, God and gin, the Sublime and the gor blimey.

Enjoy it all, but go easy on the gin.